IMAGES OF WAR
STALINGRAD

IMAGES OF WAR
STALINGRAD
VICTORY ON THE VOLGA

RARE PHOTOGRAPHS FROM WARTIME ARCHIVES

NIK CORNISH

Pen & Sword
MILITARY

First published in Great Britain in 2009 by
PEN & SWORD MILITARY
an imprint of
Pen & Sword Books Ltd,
47 Church Street, Barnsley,
South Yorkshire.
S70 2AS

ISBN 978-1-84415-934-5

A CIP catalogue record for this book is available
from the British Library

Typeset by Mac Style, Beverley, East Yorkshire
Printed and bound in Great Britain by CPI

Pen & Sword Books Ltd incorporates the imprints of
Pen & Sword Aviation, Pen & Sword Maritime,
Pen & Sword Military, Pen & Sword Select, Pen & Sword Military Classics,
Leo Cooper, Wharncliffe Local History

For a complete list of Pen & Sword titles please contact:
PEN & SWORD BOOKS LIMITED
47 Church Street, Barnsley, South Yorkshire, S70 2AS, England.
E-mail: enquiries@pen-and-sword.co.uk
Website: www.pen-and-sword.co.uk

Contents

Stalingrad: Victory on the Volga is dedicated to
my mum, Dorothy, Angie and my children,
Charlotte and Alex.

Preface

The Imperial Russian and Soviet armed forces have exercised a fascination for me since I learnt to read (in the middle of the last century) from *The Times History of the Great War* when I discovered there was someone else called Nikolas – the last Tsar of Russia! Furthermore, during my teens, I found that it was the Red Army (the bogey-man of the time) who had made the most significant contribution to the defeat of the Axis in the Second World War, not the Americans, who occasionally acknowledged limited support from Britain!

The more I read, the more I wanted to know about the eastern fronts in both World Wars. Unsurprisingly the battles of Stalingrad and Kursk featured high on the list. As accounts of the Battle of Stalingrad are now being published that take the words of veterans as their basis, more realistic pictures of events are appearing that lack the communist phraseology and cant of earlier works. Therefore I was pleased to be able to undertake this commission and draw on such sources to give a backing to the images in this work for Pen and Sword. The Soviet military and civilian images are sourced from Russian museums and archives as noted in the credit lines and many have until now been unpublished in the west. I have also collected, over a period of several years, images of German and Axis armed forces on the Eastern Front, many of which appear here.

Although the efforts and monumental sacrifices of the Red Army and the peoples of the former Soviet Union having been increasingly noted in the west any work that publicizes these facets of Twentieth Century history cannot be in vain. Therefore it is to be hoped that *Stalingrad: Victory on the Volga*, while not ground-breaking in its coverage of events, will contribute in its own modest way to further an understanding of the horrors of the Second World War on the Eastern Front.

Thanks are due to Pier Paolo Battistelli, Dmitri Belanovsky (as always), Bob Forczyk and Steve Zaloga.

Photograph Sources

Nik Cornish at Stavka
All photographs not listed below.

Courtesy of the Central Museum of the Armed Forces, Moscow
Photographs on pages 13, 14, 17 (bottom), 19 (top), 20 (top), 21, 34, 36 (bottom), 38 (bottom), 41, 44, 45, 47, 53 (top), 56 (bottom), 62, 64, 68, 70, 71, 72 (bottom), 73 (top), 74, 76, 77, 79, 87 (top), 88 (bottom), 89 (top), 90 (bottom), 91, 92, 93, 94, 95, 99, 100 (bottom), 102, 104 (top), 105 (bottom), 108, 110, 116, 117, 121 (bottom), 122 (top), 123 (bottom), 124, 126 (top), 131 (bottom), 135 (bottom), 136 (bottom), 138, 139 (bottom), 135 (bottom), 136 (bottom), 138, 139 (bottom), 146 (bottom), 147 (top), 150, 151 (bottom), 152 (top), 153, 154, 155 (bottom), 156, 157, 159, 160.

From the Fonds of the RGAKFD at Krasnogorsk
Photographs on pages 33, 38 (top), 42, 55, 58 (top), 59, 60, 84, 86, 106 (top), 118 (bottom), 120 (bottom), 132, 141, 147 (top), 158.

Introduction

On 22 June 1941 Axis forces invaded the USSR opening the war on the Eastern Front. Three formations, Army Group North, Army Group Centre and Army Group South, pushed towards Leningrad, Moscow and Ukraine respectively. Operation Barbarossa, Hitler's codename for the offensive designed to destroy the Soviet Union, was under way.

Within hours of the offensive much of the Red Air Force had been destroyed on the ground, leaving the Luftwaffe in control of the clear summer skies. On the ground the experience gained by the Panzertruppen against the Poles and the western allies delivered a series of shattering lessons in mobile warfare to the Red Army as the huge battles of encirclement bit deep into Stalin's empire. Behind the tanks and Stukas trudged the infantry, marching across the wheat-covered steppes, their progress marked by the plumes of dust rising from the unmetalled roads. In the opposite direction shuffled seemingly endless columns of Soviet POWs, their expressions dejected and shocked as they came to terms with their new situation.

It was the job of the German and other Axis infantry divisions to consolidate and secure the spectacular advances made by their more illustrious colleagues. The mopping-up of pockets of resistance, not always a simple task, as the defenders of Brest Fortress demonstrated for almost five weeks, showed that, however badly damaged the Red Army had been, it was certainly not going to roll over and capitulate. Despite reeling punch-drunk from the ferocity of the Axis offensive, the Red Army fought with desperation, throwing men and machines into almost suicidal counterattacks and holding actions wherever possible. But for all their losses, city after city fell and prisoners by the million were lost. To even the most confident of the Red Army's commanders the inexorable advance of their enemies must have appeared unstoppable.

By the end of September Kiev had fallen, the roofs of Leningrad were in sight and Moscow lay 402km beyond the front line of Army Group Centre.

During the first week of October the German High Command launched Operation Typhoon, the purpose of which was to capture Moscow and deal a killing blow to what was believed to be a virtually crippled Red Army. Over the course of the next six weeks Army Group Centre almost achieved its goal. It was at the point where victory seemed within its grasp that AGC reached the end of its tether – its supply chain was overextended and this, coupled with command errors, the increasingly appalling weather and stubborn Soviet defence, caused the tide to turn.

The Soviet counteroffensive began on 5 December and by the end of 1941 five out of six of AGC's armies were retreating in disarray as Soviet cavalry raided far and wide behind German lines, even threatening the major rail supply line from Orel. Stalin, encouraged by such successes, and against the advice of his advisors, insisted on increasing the scope of the offensive. Hitler, dismissing the doubts of many of his senior commanders, demanded that his forces hold firm, which they managed to do, but at great cost in men and material.

Army Group North, having failed to take Leningrad off the march, had taken up winter quarters and begun to develop siege lines. On 21 November Rostov on Don, regarded as the gateway to the oil and cereal wealth of the Caucasus, fell to Army Group South but a Soviet counterattack recaptured it before the end of 1941, pushing the front line back to the Mius River.

By the end of February 1942 Stalin's overly ambitious offensive had run out of steam and both sides paused to draw breath and consider their next moves.

Operation Barbarossa had begun with an overwhelming sense of optimism, as shown by the destinations written on the coach sides. Suwalki, in East Prussia, marked the jump-off point for this unit of Army Group Centre's Third Panzer Gruppe (army); Klin, less than 50km north-west of Moscow, marked its deepest penetration.

The vast, open steppes of Ukraine and southern Russia were ideal tank country. The Soviet BT-7 tank seen burning in the rear of this image symbolizes the destruction of many of the Red Army's armoured formations during the summer of 1941. The sense of numbness felt on capture is evident on the faces of the Soviet POWs.

As the troops of Army Group Centre neared Moscow the weather changed for the worse. Designed for western European conditions, many of the Wehrmacht's motor vehicles proved inadequate for the harsh environment of the USSR. Delicate western horses were replaced by hardier Russian breeds. The local *panje* wagon proved more than a match for mud and snow.

However, it was not only the harshness of the climate that stopped the Wehrmacht in its tracks outside Moscow. Seen moving through the outskirts of the Soviet capital is a T-34/76 model 1941. The broad tracks were well adapted to the snow, as were the Siberian troops who formed the backbone of Stalin's counteroffensive during the winter of 1941–42.

Ill-prepared for the viciousness of a Russian winter, the Wehrmacht fell back in the face of Soviet attacks. A patrol of Red Army men clad in their winter coveralls moves towards a recently abandoned German position in January 1942.

Amongst a park of abandoned German vehicles a Soviet engineer cautiously sweeps the area for mines. Although the Germans retreated hastily they frequently seeded their former positions with mines and booby traps. By the end of December 1941 Army Group Centre had been decisively repulsed before Moscow.

Chapter 1

Voronezh, Stalingrad or the Black Gold?

From the German perspective the origins of the Stalingrad campaign lay in the desire of Hitler to gain control of the economic resources of the Caucasus, particularly the oilfields. The failure of Operation Barbarossa to accomplish the destruction of the USSR by the end of 1941 and the losses incurred by the Wehrmacht led to a re-evaluation of the Axis position in the east. Although the forces were mainly German, Hungary, Italy and Romania had all contributed substantial numbers of men, aircraft and armoured vehicles and these were all counted on the strength of Army Group South, which held the line from Orel to the Black Sea, a distance of 805km. A thorn in Army Group South's side was the ongoing siege of Sevastopol, which tied down Manstein's Eleventh Army's considerable assets.

Hitler published his strategic overview for 1942 in Fuhrer Directive 41 on 5 April. In it he declared that Grozny, Maikop and Baku, the centres of ninety per cent of Soviet oil production, were to be the major objectives, alongside the destruction of the Red Army. With the acquisition of the cereal-producing region of the Kuban as a by-blow, Stalingrad was very much a secondary target. Convinced that the USSR was reaching the end of its capacity to wage war, Hitler also believed that the Red Army could be finally despatched with a series of encirclements repeating the successes of 1941.

The codename given to these operations was *Blau* (Blue), and it was to be a three-stage offensive. Stage one involved Second Army and Fourth Panzer Army driving towards Voronezh. The second stage, immediately to the south, would be undertaken by Sixth Army, and involved the encirclement of Soviet forces west of the upper Don River. In stage three, Fourth Panzer Army would move down the Don and link up with Seventeenth Army advancing from Rostov and then Stalingrad would fall. These were the precursors to the main attack into the Caucasus, which would then follow. Army groups North and Centre would both contribute Panzer divisions to Army Group South and remain on the defensive. However, movements, codenamed Operation Kremlin, were to be carried out in the rear of Army Group Centre to deceive the Soviet intelligence services that Moscow was the main target of the summer campaign. Immediately before Operation *Blau* began, Army Group South numbered roughly 1,000,000 German and 300,000 allied troops with the support of Air Fleet Four led by Colonel General Richthofen.

But the Soviets had not been idle. On 12 May they opened their own offensive with the twin objectives of liberating Kharkov and freeing the industrial region of the Donbass. The method chosen was simple: Timoshenko's South-Western Front would carry out a vast pincer movement. At first the Red Army made ground as the Germans had been completely taken by surprise. Within two days the Soviets' pincers had advanced 24km and 32km as the men of Sixth Army fought tenaciously to prevent their encirclement.

Paulus suggested withdrawal but Bock had more aggressive plans and on 17 May launched First Panzer Army in a counterattack against the southern face of the Barvenko Salient. Two days later Stalin agreed that the offensive be called off but it was too late. Paulus went into the attack from the north of the salient and by the end of May Soviet casualties were approaching 300,000, of whom some two-thirds were POWs mainly trapped in a series of encircling operations. However, Sixth Army returned casualty figures of 20,000, a not inconsiderable loss given the short duration of the fighting. With the sideshow at an end the Germans could now proceed with the main event – the establishment of their start line and the bridgeheads over the Don River.

On 19 June Stalin was handed a set of German documents describing the role of XL Panzer Corps in the upcoming offensive. Despite this fabulous piece of luck the Soviet leader refused to believe that Hitler's summer objective could be anything other than Moscow and therefore refused to give the papers any credence. When Army Group South, of which Paulus's Sixth Army formed the largest part, opened its attack Stalin refused to give the local commanders a free hand with the result that, despite fierce resistance, a 64km gap opened between the Bryansk and South-Western fronts within a week of the German attack. Despite several armoured counterattacks Voronezh fell and the upper Don was cut. At this point Army Group South was divided into two, Army Group B and Army Group A. With Army Group B established at Voronezh and spreading south-eastwards along the Don River, it was the turn of Army Group A.

On 16 July Hitler took a momentous decision and ordered Fourth Panzer Army to join Army Group A as the eastern arm of the encircling movement aimed at Rostov. Once again Hitler was aiming for the battle of encirclement that had eluded Army Group B and this time he anticipated it would occur during the fighting for Rostov. Again he was proved wrong; although Rostov fell on 23 July and the route to the black gold of the Caucasus lay open, the Red Army had lived to fight another day. Two days later List's men plunged into the Kuban steppe.

Hitler ordered Paulus to take Stalingrad on 20 July 1942 in the following terms: 'Thrust forward to Stalingrad, to smash the enemy forces concentrated there, to occupy the town, and block the land communications between the Don and the Volga, as well as the Don itself.' Ten days later he ordered Fourth Panzer Army to return to Army Group B along the south bank of the Don River in the direction of Stalingrad. But Paulus had been deprived of the XL Panzer Corps on 13 July and due to the perambulations of it and Fourth Panzer Army had missed the opportunity to take Stalingrad at the time when the Soviets were almost incapable of defending it.

A wrecked T-34/76 lies in the mud of the *rasputitsa*, the Russian name for the period of the thaw during which the earth turned to glutinous mud that imposed a natural break on offensive operations until the ground hardened sufficiently. Again, however, the T-34 enjoyed the advantage of wider tracks than its panzer force opponents.

Front-line Red Army men receive instruction in the use of the Degtyarev DP 7.62mm light machine-gun, six of which were issued to each rifle company. In common with all Soviet-produced weapons it adhered to the principles of being robust, simple and virtually soldier-proof. Its round disc-like magazine earned it the nickname of the 'record player'.

As the weather in the USSR improved, the thoughts of the Axis leaders turned to a renewal of the offensive in the east. Here a German 105mm howitzer crew waits for orders. The backbone of the Wehrmacht's artillery arm, the 105 had a range of 12,200m and a firing rate of eight rounds per minute.

Hundreds of Soviet factories and millions of tons of equipment were evacuated during the first six months of the war in the east. Pictured is a tank repair workshop. At the beginning of 1942, with ever increasing speed these facilities began to produce weapons and supplies of all types. Soviet industry was placed on an all-out war footing from the first weeks of the Axis invasion, unlike Germany's, which produced below capacity until 1943.

With the onset of spring and firmer terrain the forces of both sides prepared for combat. A 20mm flak unit keeps an eye to the sky over Sixth Army's front during the Soviet offensive of May 1942. The Red Air Force was still suffering from the battering its morale had taken during the previous year and was held in low esteem by the Axis.

As Sixth Army recovered from its initial shock von Bock ordered Paulus to counterattack. Soviet attacks were, at this time, still in the style of those of the First World War with waves of infantrymen charging forward. The support weapon is the Degtyarev. German memoirs record these attacks as being vodka-fuelled.

A heavy armoured car, the Sd.Kfz 233, of the Grossdeutschland Motorized Infantry Division heads eastwards. Although still weak the Red Air Force could not be discounted and wariness of air strikes has prompted the heavy camouflage. Armed with a short 75mm gun the 233 performed a support role for reconnaissance units.

Still effective against thinly armoured opposition, the Soviet PTRD 14.5mm anti-tank rifle was a popular weapon. It was operated by a two-man crew and each rifle battalion was issued with six. In the hands of a marksman it was also a lethal sniper's weapon against human targets.

Soviet POWs from Twenty-Eighth Army wait for orders. Many were recently recruited men from the liberated areas who were pressed into the army. Lacking uniforms or any identification as soldiers such recruits were often shot out of hand as, in the German parlance they were 'Bandits'. Many such volunteered for work with Axis formations to avoid such a fate.

A column of panzer mark IIIs from 23rd Panzer Division in the area of Rososha, in July 1942. The divisional symbol, the Eiffel Tower, is almost visible on the left-hand mudguard of the nearest vehicle. Extra sections of track have been added to the front armour to increase its capacity to resist Soviet gunfire.

The commander of Sixth Army was General of Panzertruppen Friedrich Paulus. A contemporary described him as 'tall, of neat appearance'. A staff officer of considerable experience, Paulus was a Hitler loyalist. Seen here observing artillery fire into Stalingrad, Paulus was outclassed by Chuikov in the art of streetfighting, but it was his men who paid the ultimate price.

Italian infantry of Gariboldi's Eighth Army move into positions along the Don River during the summer of 1942. The Italians held the left flank between Second Hungarian and Third Romanian armies. Weak in armour and anti-tank weapons, Eighth Army was supported by German XXIX Corps.

A group of Soviet POWs are escorted to the rear by men of Romania's Third Army. Although Army Groups A and B overran vast swathes of territory the number of prisoners taken was disappointingly low as a result of Stalin's change of mind and his decision to trade space for lives and equipment.

This Toldi II is one of Hungary's domestically produced armoured vehicles. Armed with a 20mm gun, it was below the standard required for front-line duties. Reconnaissance elements of Hungarian Second Army reached the Don River on 7 July having advanced 160km in ten days. Unfortunately the Soviets held three bridgeheads in Second Army's sector of the Don which were to prove invaluable during the winter counteroffensive.

Colonel General Wolfram von Richthofen (left), a relative of the Red Baron and commander of Fourth Air Fleet, is seen here about to board his personal Fieseler Storch. Richthofen's 1500 aircraft dominated the skies over southern Russia and Stalingrad until the coming of winter when flying was reduced to a minimum. Richthofen's instructions from Hitler had included the phrase 'destruction of the city of Stalingrad'.

A Panzer IV F2 of the Grossdeutschland Motorized Infantry Division armed with a long 75mm gun moves into position in the vicinity of Voronezh in July 1942. The unit's emblem, a white *Stalhelm*, can be seen on the rear mudguard. The mark IV was the workhorse of the Panzer divisions from this time until the end of the war.

Lend-Lease in action. An American M3 (General Lee) from 114 Armoured Brigade, XXIII Armoured Corps, captured from the South-Western Front. Inadequate in armour, weaponry and performance, the M3 had a poor reputation amongst Soviet tank crews. However, several were put to work for the Germans.

A member of a German engineering unit stands next to sign reading 'Here begins the arse of the world'. Conditions on the Russian steppes in summer resembled those of North Africa: lack of water, dust clogging machinery and lungs and an awe-inspiring emptiness. The roads were even less developed than those encountered in 1941 and the Axis supply network was hard pressed to keep up with demand.

Mission accomplished, an unidentified man of XLVIII Panzer Corps stands in front of what may be the central railway station in Voronezh. Unfortunately for Bock the city took four days of streetfighting to capture, finally falling on 9 July. Hitler replaced Bock with Field Marshal Weichs and altered Operation *Blau* by diverting XL Panzer Corps south-east.

Despite having conquered territory the fighting west of the Don River had not resulted in the collapse of the Soviet South-Western Front. Stalin's new Chief of Staff, Colonel General Vasilevsky, had prevailed upon him to alter Soviet strategy and trade space for men and machines. The prolonged fighting at Voronezh allowed South-Western and Southern fronts to avoid encirclement from the north. Here armour and artillery of Field Marshal List's Army Group A engage Soviet forces in the northern Caucasus.

Chapter 2

Order 227

In Moscow Stalin had also been reviewing his plans in the light of Moscow no longer seeming to be the Axis' target. On 12 July the Stalingrad Front was established from the remains of the South-Western Front and other units in the area. A week later the city was placed on a war footing.

Stalingrad had been rebuilt as a model industrial city during the 1930s. Workers' homes and factories had been arranged for ease of access and to provide a pleasant living area. Running along the west bank of the Volga River for some 40km, it was an attractive place to live for its population of 400,000; however, it is estimated that refugees had added some 250,000 to that number. The larger factories were to the north of the city, backing in places onto the steep banks of the river. At some points the Volga was almost a mile wide. As there was no bridge a number of ferries operated from the Main Landing Stage near Stalingrad's Red Square. From 20 July the ferries were under the control of the NKVD, who searched zealously for deserters and 'saboteurs'. Parallel to the river a railway ran the length of the city serving commuters and factories alike. Buildings were a mix of low-rise workers' flats, stone and cement-built factories and other buildings but with a large number of wooden, one-storied dwellings. Scattered everywhere were allotments, public parks, orchards and wide streets. But dominating the whole was the 102m-high Tartar burial mound known as the Mamayev Kurgan to the south of the city centre. Out on the steppe the gently undulating ground was virtually treeless and broken by *balkas*, dried-up gullies and ravines varying from at least two metres deep and up to six metres wide, which provided ready-made trenches, water barriers or anti-tank ditches. The *Tsaritsa* (yellow in Tartar) River flowed into the city at ninety degrees to the Volga, which it met near the Main Landing Stage.

A Defence Committee was established and plans were made to fortify the outskirts. The population was mobilized to dig anti-tank ditches, bunkers and protective earthworks around the riverside oil and petrol tanks. Those living out on the steppe were ordered to abandon their homes on the pretext that the Red Army could use them as defensive positions. However, the reality was political; the local and central authorities were concerned that the Cossacks of the Don steppe would support the Germans and provide them with food, but more importantly, intelligence and recruits. Those who refused to leave their homes were denounced as traitors. In the city factory workers were organized into Special Brigades and female members of the Komsomol were trained as anti-aircraft gunners.

As July drew to an end the situation west of Stalingrad deteriorated. Two armies, Sixty-Second and Sixty-Fourth, had been shattered almost to the point of collapse. Concerned that the Red Army needed more stick than carrot, Stalin issued Order 227 on 28 July. There was an honest appraisal of the situation detailing losses of territory, population and economic assets. This was followed by a comparison between the situation of the Axis forces before Moscow in 1941, and how severe disciplinary measures had been imposed to save them, and the condition of the South-Western Front presently. In short, Stalin declared:

> This leads to the conclusion; it is time to finish retreating. Not one step back [...] It is impossible to tolerate commanders and commissars who admit that some panic mongers determined the situation on the field of combat [...] panic mongers and cowards should be exterminated in place [... those] who retreat without orders from higher commanders are betrayers of the motherland.

The order concluded with several clear instructions to unit commanders to form blocking detachments to ensure that men did not leave their positions and for these detachments to enforce strict discipline – shoot deserters there and then. And for those who showed a less than enthusiastic attitude there were to be penal companies where they could redeem themselves – if they survived.

However, the Germans did not pause in their advance to allow the Soviets to absorb Stalin's words. Army Group A had by 9 August reached Krasnodar in the heart of the Kuban cereal-producing region and Maikop in the foothills of the Caucasus Mountains. At Maikop the oilfields had been comprehensively ruined forcing the First Panzer Army to depend even more on Luftwaffe supply drops and a land supply line that mixed rail, lorry and mule transport. As List's advance slowed to a snail's pace due to supply problems and increasingly effective Soviet defensive tactics, so Hitler's interest in Stalingrad grew from interest to obsession.

Sixth Army faced Sixty-Second and Sixty-Fourth armies and although both Soviet formations were in a poor condition and in danger of separation, Vasilevsky realized that they could not be withdrawn and must be supported if the Sixth Army avalanche was to be held up. Therefore a counterattack by First Tank Army was launched. The gamble paid off and Paulus was forced onto the defensive. Meanwhile to the south of Stalingrad Fourth Panzer Army launched its attack on the city, facing Fifty-First Army, which linked Sixty-Fourth Army to the Volga River: it too was forced onto the defensive.

Both sides took breath during this stand-off during the first week of August. A new Soviet front was created, South-Eastern, which controlled Stalingrad from the south as far as the Tsaritsa River; north from there was the purview of Stalingrad Front itself. Simultaneously Weichs ordered Sixth and Fourth Panzer armies to mount a concentric attack on the Soviets west of the city. Sixth Army would cross the Don and Fourth Panzer would reach the Volga. By 23 August leading elements of Sixth Army had crossed the Don and 16th Panzer Division had covered the 80km to the banks of the Volga just north of Stalingrad. But Fourth Panzer Army had not made such startling progress and for six days 16th Panzer Division fought hard to maintain its position. Finally Fourth Panzer Army linked up with Sixth Army at Pitomnik, 15km to the west of Stalingrad. But once again a great encirclement had been evaded by the

Red Army as both Sixty-Second and Sixty-Fourth armies withdrew to the outskirts. 16th Panzer Division was relieved and by the end of August Sixth Army closed up to the Volga only to be met by a Soviet counterattack on its left flank. As the Soviets attacked Paulus they were unable to break through. And as Fourth Panzer Army linked up with Paulus's LI Corps Sixty-Second Army pulled back into the city proper.

The stage was now set for the epic battle of attrition that was the fighting for the ruins of Stalingrad itself.

Red Army machine-gunners wait for a German attack. The immaculate uniforms and the solid position suggest that this is a posed image despite an original caption extolling the bravery of the men of the Sixty-Fourth Army during the summer of 1942.

A KV-1 heavy tank breaks cover during a counterattack. Following one such unsuccessful counterattack the wrecks of burned-out KV tanks were likened to a field of elephants. By the end of August the opportunities for such operations were coming to an end as both sides focussed on the fighting for the city of Stalingrad itself.

Men of 24th Panzer Division struggle to move their vehicles forward through the sandy ground. Part of Sixth Army, 24th Panzer had been a cavalry unit until January 1942 when it had been converted into an armoured formation. Its advanced units cut the Stalingrad–Morozovsk railway line on 31 August.

The shattered hulk of a BP-35 Soviet armoured train called 'For the Motherland' destroyed by an air strike on Fourth Panzer Army's front. The Red Army had dozens of such behemoths and used them often with great gusto. This version incorporates the turrets of KV-2 and T-34 tanks as well as a 75mm gun and several machine-guns.

A remarkable image of burning house in the workers' residential area of Red October in the centre of the city. The two-day blitz of the city lasted from 23 to 24 August and caused over 30,000 casualties. The civilian and military authorities just about managed to maintain order. The evacuation of women and children increased in pace after this, hampered only by the evacuation of wounded men, who retained priority.

A Stuka crew prepares for a mission. Operating from grass airfields, such as this one at Kalach on the Don River's eastern bank and within 80km of the target, was a pleasant experience for the air and ground crews alike despite the occasional sortie by the Red Air Force. Stukas were equipped with sirens to be used to increase their victims' fear as they dived to drop their bomb loads.

The Fourth Air Fleet's first terror raids on Stalingrad caused mayhem. Starting on Sunday 23 August wave after wave of Stukas, Junkers 88s and Heinkel IIIs swept over the city. Incendiary bombs caused the wooden buildings to burn like chaff. Here a group of children sit glumly amidst the ruins of their neighbourhood. The fate of their parents was not recorded by the correspondent.

The anti-aircraft defences of the city were split between both banks of the river and priority was given to defending the factory districts and strategic assets such as the power station. Many batteries were manned by female students, some of whom turned their guns on German tanks when such targets presented themselves. Here a male crew operates the standard Soviet AA gun 85mm model 1939. Unfortunately many batteries had not received ammunition when the raids began.

Mountain artillerymen of 1st Mountain Division in action near the Caucasian foothills. A combined group from this and 4th Mountain Division planted the Nazi flag at the summit of Mount Elbrus, a propaganda coup but strategically worthless. In early September Hitler sacked List and took personal command of Army Group A. However, despite the Fuhrer's exhortations, little further advance was made.

A Panzer II stands guard over an abandoned Soviet munitions train which appears to have a cargo of anti-aircraft guns. Allegedly this image shows the Stalingrad–Morozovsk railway, where, briefly, Paulus had an opportunity to cut off the remnants of Sixty-Second and Sixty-Fourth armies. However, the moment passed.

Caucasian natives ride in to meet German forces during August–September 1942. Thousands of the local tribesmen saw the Axis as liberators from the Russian/Communist yoke and offered themselves as volunteer combatants. When the Soviets undertook the reconquest of the northern Caucasus the NKVD under the Georgian Beria undertook a particularly vicious campaign of mass murder and deportation against those who did not retreat with their Axis employers.

A Soviet counterattack with tank desant troops goes in under cover of an early morning mist. This was probably one of the Soviet attacks on XIV Panzer Corps along the flanks of the corridor to Rynok undertaken by First Guards and Twenty-Fourth armies. These attacks held XIV Panzer in place at great cost but saved Sixty-Second and Sixty-Fourth armies from envelopment.

Dug in beside a carefully draped German corpse, infantry of the Red Army keep watch over an empty, featureless piece of steppe. During the summer of 1942 Soviet propaganda had taken an increasingly nationalistic and emotional line. Sidelined were the appeals to fight for the party and world revolution; the emphasis was now on national survival and the vicious, inhumane behaviour of the German invaders.

An 88mm anti-aircraft gun prepares for action against a ground target. The 88 was quite capable of destroying any of the Soviet tanks fielded up to this time. The gun's high profile and the need to remove its wheels to deploy made it an easy target if its crew were caught unawares. The crew here have taken the profile into account, attempting to lose the gun in the buildings to the rear.

Men and vehicles of 16th Panzer Division prepare for another day on the baking steppe. Theirs was the first German unit to reach the Volga River, the suburb of Rynok, on 23 August. Here they were engaged by anti-aircraft batteries crewed by female students from the city's university. The German report paid tribute to the Russian girls when their position had fallen, describing them as 'tenacious'.

Worker volunteers for the militia 'Special Brigades' that were formed from those employed in factories not connected with the munitions industry. Placed under the command of 10th NKVD Division, these men were sent into battle against the veterans of Sixth Army with predictable results. Here they receive instruction in the workings of a Mosin-Nagant rifle, the standard infantry weapon of the Red Army. Many had to rely on picking up guns from fallen comrades.

One of the *balkas*, or water courses, that criss-crossed the steppes to the west of Stalingrad. Towards the top of the image a man can be seen, giving an idea of the balka's dimensions. Such natural tank traps proved to be the downfall of many a careless panzer driver.

One of the last cities of importance to fall to the Axis was the Black Sea port of Novorossisk. Here Romanian infantry storm one of the last Soviet barricades before the waterfront. Third Romanian Army had made excellent progress along the eastern coast of the Black Sea but Novorossisk marked the end of their advance. The city was taken on 10 September, but also marked the limit of Army Group A's capabilities.

Men of the Sixty-Second Army pull back into suburban Stalingrad. It was cut off from Sixty-Fourth Army to the south when the German 29th Motorized Division drove through to the Volga River at the suburb of Kuporosnoye on 10 September.

A charmingly posed shot of Russian villagers who have turned out to work on a railway line near their home village during the summer of 1942. Stalin had authorized the building of an alternative rail link some 25km east of Stalingrad. Speed restrictions were necessary due to the poor quality of the work. Nevertheless it worked and provided a vital supply line to the city during the fighting. Not all the inhabitants of the plains west of Stalingrad were as obedient as these ladies. Memories, particularly amongst the Don Cossack population, were of the Communist repression during the years following 1919.

Chapter 3

Backs to the Volga

With 16th Panzer Division shelling boats on the Volga River and 29th Motorized Division doing the same south of the city while the Luftwaffe roamed both banks at will, the river was obviously cut by the first week of September. Sixty-Second Army commanded by General Lopatin had managed to retreat into the city environs. Yeremenko, commander of the Stalingrad Front, had established his HQ in the gorge through which the Tsaritsa River flowed into the Volga, roughly 900m south of the Main Landing Stage and twice that distance from Railway Station 1 (Stalingrad's main station) and the city's Red Square. The question faced by Yeremenko and political commissar the Ukrainian (and later leader of the USSR) Nikita Khrushchev was, who should command Sixty-Second Army, as Lopatin was judged to be defeatist. General Vasily Chuikov was the man chosen. On 12 September Chuikov took command in Stalingrad. As the front HQ was evacuated to the eastern bank he hurried to his command post at the foot of the Mamayev Kurgan Tartar burial mound, which commanded the city in all directions and was a strategic point of the utmost value to both sides.

The Soviet forces in the city numbered some 20,000 on the strength of Sixty-Second Army and roughly 10,000 militia and others, the remains of devastated units that had drifted in during the last first week of September. These men and a mixed bag of sixty or so tanks and 700 guns and mortars held a semicircular position from Rynok in the north to Kuporosnoye in the south, a line of roughly 87km that still encompassed some open ground to the west.

On the day that Chuikov reached his new HQ Paulus was at Vinnitsa in Ukraine telling an increasingly agitated Hitler that he could take Stalingrad following 'ten days of fighting'. Hitler had become dissatisfied with the Wehrmacht's performance in the Caucasus during August. Now, as it became evident that the capture of the oilfields of that region would be beyond the resources allocated for the task, he became increasingly fixated on taking Stalingrad. Paulus regrouped and resupplied his forces during the first half of September with the intention of attacking the city itself on 13 September.

Sixth Army comprised fifteen divisions. Strecker's XI Corps covered the approaches to the city, guarding against Fourth Tank and Twenty-First armies across on the northern bank of the Don River. On its right flank lay VIII Corps and XIV Panzer Corps. The line was continued by the five divisions of LI Corps under von Seydlitz-Kurzbach. South of the Tsaritsa River lay Fourth Panzer Army led by Colonel General Hermann Hoth, which included 24th and 14th Panzer divisions as well as 94th Infantry and 29th Motorized divisions. Hoth's other two infantry divisions, 297th and 371st, covered the right flank of Sixty-Fourth Army.

The honour of opening the attack fell to Seydlitz-Kurzbach's men. The 295th Infantry drove straight up the slopes of the Mamayev Kurgan, while two others pushed towards the Main Landing Stage and Railway Station 1 in the city centre. Throughout the morning the fighting ebbed and flowed all along the line. On the Mamayev Kurgan 112th Rifle Division watched as the German attack moved towards them. Aware that around him 'Everything was roaring and burning,' as one Soviet veteran recalled, 'We tried to return their fire, but more and more of them were arriving.'

Finally weight of numbers, firepower, saturation bombing and determination drove the Soviet infantry from the Mamayev Kurgan and back towards the built-up areas. At 13.00 hrs the war diary of Sixty-Second Army recorded the Mamayev's fall. Elsewhere the news was equally gloomy. To the south two German infantry divisions had, by midday, reached Railway Station 1 and captured the waterworks. Chuikov transferred his HQ to a balka on the northern bank of the Tsaritsa River. It was there he received the commander of 13th Guards Rifle Division, General Rodimtsev, and Colonel Sarayev, the city's garrison commander and commander of 10th NKVD Rifle Division. Sarayev was ordered to use his workers' militia battalions to secure strategic locations and deploy his NKVD infantry in support. This was a remarkable situation as the NKVD was independent of the Red Army. However, Sarayev agreed and replied, 'I am now a soldier of Sixty-Second Army.' Chuikov now had sole control of the city's defences. But he desperately needed more men, as the Germans were streaming along the ruined streets with their armour, adding to the confusion by sporting Soviet markings. With the Mamayev in German hands it was essential that Chuikov counterattack and regain it but to do this he needed to retain the Main Landing Stage to ferry in reserves. Already disillusioned and shell-shocked, Russian troops had begun to desert or to abandon their positions.

A further blow had been struck to morale when Chuikov ordered all his heavy artillery to be moved to the eastern bank of the Volga: 'Everyone took this as a sign that Stalingrad was about to be abandoned.'

The 13th Guards Division had originally been scheduled to cross into the city during the night. However, the situation was now so critical that its move was brought forward to late afternoon. But first the quays had to be secured as the Germans were within 1000m of Chuikov's HQ and not much further from the quays. A scratch group of tanks and HQ staff was assembled and tasked with the defence of the quays. At the same time Rodimtsev was addressing the advance guard of his division and explaining the desperate situation across the river. Battalions from 39 Guards and 42 Guards regiments crossed the river under continual aerial, mortar and small arms fire. Boat after boat was holed and soon the Volga ran red, but the survivors hit the banks and attacked up the slopes, heedless of casualties. Taken by surprise, the Germans gave ground, losing control of several buildings and their dominance of the quays in the process. Rodimtsev made the crossing with the first wave and organized the area's defences as night fell and more of his division were ferried in.

A Guards' reconnaissance battalion was despatched to recapture Railway Station 1, which it succeeded in doing although the station fell again within a few days. Despite this setback Paulus's men had come within an ace of cutting Sixty-Second Army's supply line and achieving victory. Chuikov now had to take back the Mamayev before the Germans could bring up their artillery or get too well dug in.

As Paulus took stock and regrouped he could feel that Stalingrad was within his grasp. Hoth's XLVIII Panzer Corps had advanced into the southern flank, almost isolating the immense concrete grain silo and elevator. To the north progress had been made towards the industrial areas.

At 09.00 hrs on 16 September an under-strength tank brigade, a weak regiment of 112th Rifle Division and 39 Guards Regiment prepared to take the Mamayev Kurgan by storm. The attack was reminiscent of the First World War, with infantry rushing trenches and machine-guns. Again Rodimtsev was there to inspire his men as they charged. With some artillery cover they rushed up the slopes towards the German trenches. By 11.00 hrs the Red Flag was flying over the summit of the Mamayev.

From 15 to 21 September fighting for the grain silo held up the advance of Fourth Panzer Army, and when it finally fell, the southern side of the Main Landing Stage was also under fire. One infantry division, an infantry brigade and a brigade of naval infantry had defended this section of the line but were so weakened that they were amalgamated into 92 Brigade.

Chuikov had once again moved his HQ, this time to the riverbank behind the Red October factory. Unfortunately he lacked good communications with 92 Brigade. However, despite many of the men and a large number of senior officers leaving their positions, the 92nd held on, covering the left flank of 13th Guards. It was not until 22 September when the Germans launched another ferocious attack that the brigade finally broke. The gap was plugged by men of 13th Guards but the period that they had spent in the city had reduced their number from 10,000 to less than 1000. Happily for Sixty-Second Army, two more divisions crossed during the next week. However, in Moscow, discussions were being held and plans laid for a new offensive, not simply aimed at relieving the pressure on Stalingrad's hard-pressed defenders but something far more ambitious – the destruction of Sixth Army itself.

German infantry of 29th Motorized Division make their way towards the smoking remains of southern Stalingrad. It is probable that this is the Yelshanka district. One of their number recorded seeing the German flag flying over the city centre on 16 September.

Another shattered Soviet tank, a KV-1, marks the progress of the German advance into the city. Not all areas had, during the early days of September, suffered such comprehensive destruction as some. The main value of armour such as this was as mobile pillboxes providing machine-gun and artillery support, as their mobility was limited in the city itself.

German artillery opens fire on Stalingrad at 04.45 hrs Berlin time on 13 September. Inevitably there was counterbattery fire but this unit has taken little pain to conceal its position from aerial observation. The gun in action is a 210mm howitzer with a range of 16.7km.

In the open spaces along the banks of the Orlovka River a Soviet rations party goes to ground as the German shells explode nearby. Close by are some of the mobile chevaux-de-frise wire entanglements favoured by Russian engineers. Chuikov was disparaging of the field works erected around the city; Paulus was not. German reports noted 'strong positions with deep bunkers and concrete emplacements'.

A Soviet artillery bunker, one of dozens scattered throughout Stalingrad's suburbs, points westward. The concealed weapon is probably a 76mm field gun from 1902 modified in the 1930s. Dozens of such pieces had been brought out of storage and were utilized in fixed positions such as this. Chuikov described the city's defences as being based 'on blood more than barbed wire'.

After weeks of marching and fighting across open, dusty steppe German infantry of 295th Infantry Division no longer present the immaculate figures so beloved of propaganda images. However, they were the first German unit to raise the flag in the city when they captured the summit of the Mamayev Kurgan.

Grimly determined, this LMG crew, dug in on the Mamayev Kurgan, awaits the attention of German 295th Infantry Division. Possibly these are men of 33rd Guards. In peacetime the Mamayev had been part of the water supply system. At the top were four huge concrete cisterns. These cisterns provided a fine target for the Stukas.

German infantry advance past the smouldering remains of a government building. In the more open areas of the city, as here, the Germans moved confidently. However, as the combat zone became more congested with ruins, and casualties from Russian snipers mounted, their progress became markedly more cautious.

Red Army machine-gunners scurry from position to position pulling their 1910 model Maxim machine-gun on its wheeled trolley. 13th Guards Division had to rush support to the army's left flank when 92 Brigade collapsed on 22 September.

A German mortar crew, with token camouflage decorating their helmets, prepares to fire in support of an attack on the Mamayev Kurgan. The effects of air and heavy artillery strikes were negated by the close combat nature of the fighting on the Mamayev.

A remarkable shot from the nose of a Heinkel III as it begins a bombing run lining up over the Volga River, which can just be seen through the nose. Many of the Luftwaffe's efforts were concentrated on the river to interdict resupply. With little in the way of anti-aircraft fire to contend with, attacks on river traffic became something of a sport.

A Soviet MiG-3 banks to intercept a German attack. Eighth Air Army had responsibility for the Stalingrad area. Both Stalin and Khrushchev had sons in this formation. The MiG-3 provided a weak opponent for the Me-109s it faced, as it was difficult to fly and could be an unstable gun platform. Stalin's son, Vasily, commanded a unit of fighters but his formation's performance was described as 'revolting', as it had not 'shot down a single German' during early September.

Grouped near a remarkably well-preserved building, men of 100th Jager Division prepare to go on a combat patrol into the Orlovka Salient. The salient overhung Sixth Army's position and was a source of concern to Paulus. The 100th Jager was an Austrian division but included the 369th Infantry Regiment raised from Croatian collaborators. On 24 September the Croatian puppet ruler, Ante Pavelic, visited this unit to distribute medals.

Hauling the gun behind them, men of 284th Rifle Division pick their way through the chaos just above the Main Landing Stage on 24/25 September. Only light regimental or anti-tank guns were allowed into the city due to the conditions and the need to move artillery rapidly. The legendary sniper Vasily Zaitsev was a member of this division. The lead unit of this division had gone into action on 23 September – Paulus's fifty-second birthday. They swiftly gained a reputation as excellent urban fighters.

Men of 95th Rifle Division read letters from home while waiting to make the crossing into Stalingrad on the night of 16 September. It was Soviet policy to drip-feed reinforcements to Sixty-Second Army to allow for reserves to be built up elsewhere. Furthermore, conditions at the crossing points were such that larger numbers queuing up would have presented the Luftwaffe with a magnificent target.

German anti-tank gunners cheer the downing of a Soviet fighter plane. Luftwaffe pilots were discouraged from engaging in dogfights unless absolutely necessary, as their priority was specified ground targets or the ferries, troop concentrations on the eastern bank or landing areas. Happily for the pilots of Luftflotte IV's constituent units Fliegerkorps IV and VIII, Soviet opposition was at first lacklustre.

A wounded guardsman is evacuated by main force from the killing ground of the Mamayev Kurgan. By late September the ground was so chewed up by shells and bombs that one veteran remembered moving corpses so that he could sit down. The courage of the medical services on both sides was remarkable given the close proximity of the front lines.

As the Germans advanced into the city the war on the Slav 'sub-humans' was not forgotten. Sixth Army was accompanied by Sonderkommando 4a, which was responsible for the execution of Communists, Commissars and Jews. On 2 September Hitler ordered the city to be cleared of civilians. Having carried out their mission they left the Stalingrad area during the last week of September. Civilian deportations began less than a week later. Lodged in the open air, thousands died of exposure, disease and starvation.

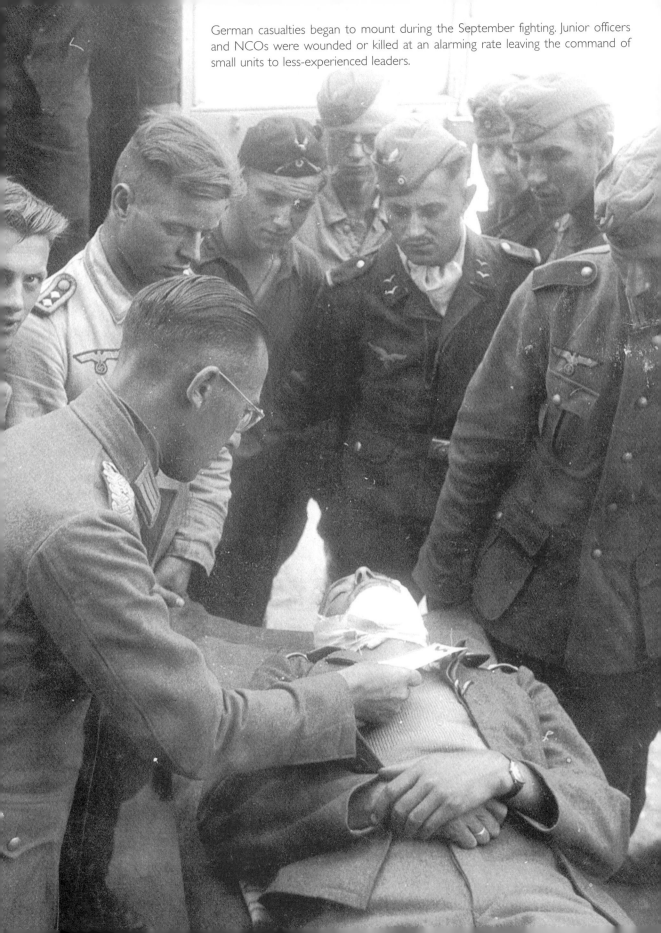

German casualties began to mount during the September fighting. Junior officers and NCOs were wounded or killed at an alarming rate leaving the command of small units to less-experienced leaders.

A dramatic image of leading elements of Rodimtsev's 13th Guards Division beginning to cross the Volga at 17.00 hrs on 14 September. The guardsmen were ordered to abandon everything but weapons and a minimum of food. Anything that could float was requisitioned and put to work. The men disembarked and charged straight into action on the opposite bank.

Chapter 4

Adapting to Circumstances

During the last week of September the staff of Sixth Army drew up plans for the second major offensive that it was hoped would take Stalingrad. This time the major objectives would be to the north and centre of the city. In essence two pincers were to break through, touch the Volga then, turning inwards, would move down the riverbank, surrounding and destroying the Soviets pinned by frontal attacks.

The southern pincer would attack from the direction of the Mamayev Kurgan towards the Red October factory, the northern pincer from the Gorodische area towards the Tractor factory. The pinning attacks would be directed towards the Barrikady factory. Having failed to take Stalingrad earlier in the month Paulus was under increasing pressure from Hitler who, frustrated by the lack of success in the Caucasus, was increasingly focussed on taking Stalin's city.

However, German preparations, the movement of so many men and so much materiel, did not go unnoticed by Chuikov's intelligence officers. Therefore Chuikov reorganized his defences. He installed the newly arrived 284th Siberian Rifle Division on the southern flank of the Mamayev to the left of 95th Rifle Division in preparation for a pre-emptive spoiling attack. Concluding his Order Number 116, Chuikov instructed officers, 'of all units and formations not to carry out operations in battle by whole units like companies and battalions. The offensive should be organized chiefly on the basis of small groups, with tommy guns, hand grenades, bottles of incendiary mixture and anti-tank rifles.'

Chuikov had reached these conclusions during the course of the previous week of fighting. At considerable risk to himself he visited the front line, spoke to the men and officers alike and, most importantly, listened and thought. To Chuikov it was clear that German successes to date had depended on the close co-operation of aircraft, artillery, infantry and armour. This worked magnificently out on the open steppe but, as the combat zone became increasingly urban, such practices were no longer as effective. German armour hesitated to attack without infantry support for fear of ambush and vice versa, and neither arm was confident when air cover was lacking. To negate the power of air and artillery strikes Chuikov ordered his men to maintain their positions as close as possible to those of the Germans, reasoning that artillery and bomber strikes would be as likely to hit their own side or be curtailed.

To increase the offensive effectiveness of his infantry he evolved what became known as Shock Groups, some 80 men divided into three sections.

The first section infiltrated and attacked an enemy position. The second section would complete the attack and secure a perimeter. The third group, roughly forty men, would then either reinforce the attack or secure the position. Members of these three sections rotated through each to gain an overall picture of the unit's roles and tactical operations. Such groups were composed of infantry, machine-gunners and engineers. Their arsenal consisted of submachine-guns, grenades, mines, extemporized trench weapons such as sharpened spades, clubs and all manner of edged weapons as well as various light and heavy machine-guns, mortars and flamethrowers if deemed necessary. A Shock Group had to be prepared to hold a position for up to 24 hours – independently. No-man's-land was to extend no further than a man could throw a hand grenade.

It is interesting to note that similar units had been raised by the Tsarist army during 1915, when they were known as Grenadier Platoons. Doubtless Chuikov, from his studies at the Frunze Military Academy during the 1920s, would have been aware of them.

Unfortunately for Chuikov's two attacking divisions new tactics did not save them from being pulverized by German air and artillery strikes as they formed up for their attack on the Mamayev Kurgan early on 27 September. An hour-long bombardment followed by an infantry attack on the German lines failed badly, both divisions taking heavy casualties. Then the Sixth Army struck back. 295th Infantry Division renewed the fighting on the Mamayev. 71st Infantry Division moved on the Red October factory and 76th Infantry division held positions around Railway Station 1. By the end of the day, 100th Jager Division had pushed to the edge of the Red October Garden City – the factory's residential area. The Germans had advanced some two miles and destroyed the greater part of two Soviet divisions in 24 hours. Furthermore it was obvious that Paulus's attack on the Orlovka Salient was about to begin. The gravity of the situation was not lost on the Soviet High Command, the Stavka, in Moscow. To ease the command and control structure in the region the defence of the city was given over to the Stalingrad Front (a Front was the equivalent of a German army group) under General Yeremenko; the old Stalingrad Front north of the city became the Don Front under General Rokossovsky, who lost no time launching a series of diversionary attacks on Sixth Army's left flank, but to no avail.

Chuikov's request for reinforcements came in the shape of 193rd Rifle Division, who took up positions in the Red October and Barrikady factories.

On 29 September Paulus unleashed his main attack on the Orlovka Salient. From the north 16th Panzer and 60th Motorized divisions pushed towards 389th and 100th Jager divisions. Part of 24th Panzer Division, transferred from south of the Tsaritsa River, fought its way towards the Barrikady and Red October areas. On the Mamayev Kurgan vicious fighting continued. Everywhere the Soviets gave ground as the weight of the relentless German thrusts drove them back. As the casualty lists rose Sixty-Second Army buckled but it did not break.

More reserves, some 10,000 men, crossed the Volga during the night of 29/30 September. Shuffling his defences, Chuikov concentrated on defending the Main Landing Stage. Fighting continued all along the 19km line held by Sixty-Second Army but the Germans made little progress. On 2 October Chuikov's HQ was almost destroyed by a cascade of blazing oil from a burst tank on the cliff above it.

Inexorably the fighting drew nearer to the Volga and further reserves arrived, parts of 37th Naval Guards Division, 84 Tank Brigade with a mixture of KV-1s, T-34s and T-60 light tanks, which were ferried over on barges. The marines were sent to the Tractor factory supported by the armour on their right. Munitions workers, still at their lathes and benches, were told to prepare for battle and organized into Special Brigades under NKVD control.

On 3 October Paulus moved the remainder of 14th Panzer and 94th Infantry divisions further to the north, as the southern suburbs were relatively quiet. The same day 112th Rifle

Division was pushed back from the Mechetka River towards the Tractor factory, just as 308th Rifle Division fell back to the perimeter of the Barrikady factory, aligning itself with 193rd Rifle Division. Fighting desperately the Russians again gave ground but the line remained intact.

The task of 14th Panzer and 94th Infantry divisions was simple; to destroy the Soviet 193rd and 308th Rifle divisions. With massive air support 14th Panzer overran the Silikat factory; however, the sting was taken from 94th Infantry's move when a powerful artillery bombardment from across the Volga broke up its attacking battalions in their assembly points. Precious time had been gained for the Soviet infantry to entrench themselves in the growing devastation of the industrial areas.

Chuikov attempted a counterattack but its effects were neutralized when 14th Panzer and 60th Motorized divisions took the housing estate belonging to the Tractor factory.

To prevent any further loss of ground as the situation was suddenly deteriorating rapidly, Chuikov ordered all the Katyusha batteries within range to launch their rockets against the assembling battalions of 60th Motorized Division. Remarkably for such an erratic weapon the shoot was good and caused significant casualties. Consequently the pressure on 37th Naval Guards and 112th Rifle divisions was relieved. Although minor local attacks continued in an attempt by both sides to create a dominant position for themselves, Paulus had shot his second bolt and still Sixty-Second Army clung to the banks of the Volga, albeit on a reduced scale.

The weather had begun to deteriorate and the nights became noticeably colder, much to the discomfort of the Germans and their allies out on the steppe. Ominously, on 25 September Fifty-First and Fifty-Seventh armies had attacked Romanian positions to the south of Stalingrad and gained some ground. Equally, if not more immediately worrying for Paulus was the casualty bill. The War Diary of 94th Infantry Division noted a front-line strength of 535, less than seventy men of all ranks per battalion. It must be said the Soviets were in no better condition.

The paratroopers of 37th Guards Division had a reputation for élan and cleanliness as well as their toughness in combat. Veterans remember them for being cleanshaven and tidy under the most difficult of conditions. During the fighting in the factory district the division suffered horrific casualties.

The German and Axis press corps were frequent visitors to the Stalingrad theatre and the use of posed images such as this for domestic consumption were not uncommon. It claims to show 'The attack on the worker's housing complex before the Tractor factory.' From that we can surmise it is supposedly the 60th Motorized Division. An unlikely camera angle.

An MG-34 team take up a support position as men of 76th Infantry Division move away from Railway Station 1. That the weapon is not in the continual fire mode suggests they will follow up. Small actions such as this were a daily occurrence in the quieter sectors of the line as each side vied to occupy advantageous positions.

A mortar team belonging to 112th Rifle Division poses for the camera during a lull in the fighting for the Orlovka Salient. The piece is an 82mm battalion weapon. It is likely that the six-man crew would move as soon as they had fired their weapon to avoid counterbattery fire.

A signature Russian weapon, the 1910 Maxim water-cooled machine-gun on its Sokolov wheeled mount. Although a good, reliable machine-gun for semi-permanent positions, the Maxim was heavy and the Storm Groups replaced it with the 'Record Player', the Degtyarev, which was air-cooled and unlikely to freeze as the weather grew colder. This weapon is positioned near the Tractor factory.

Combat engineers of 284th Infantry Division attempt to burn out a stubborn Soviet position on the Mamayev Kurgan with flamethrowers. The teams operating such weapons immediately became the target for any opponents within range.

Heavy artillery on the eastern bank prepares to zero in on German assembly positions adjacent to the Tractor factory. The gun is a 152mm piece with a range of 17,000m, more than enough to hit most targets in Stalingrad. Served by a crew of nine, it was capable of three to four rounds per minute.

Obviously taken from above, this remarkable image of part of the leading section of a Storm Group crawling to carry out a reconnaissance sweep captures the essence of urban warfare, the possibility of death lurking behind a heap of shattered masonry.

Nebelwerfers fire a barrage in support of the 94th Infantry Division's abortive assault on the gap between the Tractor and Barrikady factories on 3 October. Nicknamed 'Moaning Minnie' by the Germans, it was known to the Russians as 'Goofy'.

Anti-tank rifles in use as anti-aircraft weapons on the riverbank. One crew claimed to have shot down three Stukas. This story became part of the cult of heroism that grew up around the Sixty-Second Army. Ordinary soldiers were lauded in the press, as was the entire Sixty-Second Army, as Stalin changed the emphasis of the war from politics to nationalism.

With the Volga at his back a Luftwaffe POW is held for the camera. By early October the support given by Luftflotte IV was diminishing although the majority of its resources were being deployed over the Stalingrad area. There were simply not enough airworthy machines to interrupt Volga and east-bank traffic and simultaneously provide the requisite level of ground-attack missions.

As the consumption of munitions in Stalingrad rose, so it became essential to improve the rail links to ensure the supply chain was maintained. The main supply depot was situated at Kalach on the Don River.

Naval infantry of an unidentified unit prepare to cross the Volga River, possibly men of 37th Naval Guards Division. The vessels were under the command of Rear Admiral Rogachev who, along with his men, is amongst Stalingrad's unsung heroes. Millions of rounds of ammunition, countless tons of supplies, thousands of wounded, divisions of replacements and 200,000 civilians were shipped across the river during his tenure. Casualties amongst the Volga Flotilla's officers and men as well as their volunteer civilian crews have not been published.

Soviet entrenchments were usually considerably narrower than that shown here. However, as the original caption notes it is in a shell hole, this is unsurprising.

When the Main Landing Stage in the city centre became untenable, other crossing points were created. One of these, known as 62nd for obvious reasons, ran from Zaitsevski Island to the shore below the Red October factory. The island was connected to the eastern bank by a pontoon bridge shown here under repair and heavy fire. It was this crossing point that was used by 37th Guards (parachute) Division during the night of 3/4 October.

Men of 112th Rifle Division crawl forward as the Orlovka Salient is reduced. A semi-rural area where the Mechetka River flowed at almost a right angle into the Volga, the salient was finally overrun by 7 October, straightening the line and decreasing the frontage of Paulus's northern flank divisions considerably.

Mutually supportive, a StuG III assault gun and a section of infantry move forward during the early days of October. Assault guns were designed to operate against defensive positions; however, their gun was under-powered for damaging stronger buildings. Lacking an integral machine-gun, they were prime targets for adventurous Soviet tank-hunting teams.

Behind the lines men of 94th Infantry Division recover in the relative tranquillity of the newly occupied Orlovka Salient.

Men of various units rush down to the Volga to rescue the victims of a direct hit by a Stuka. The pall of smoke hanging over all was a constant feature when the wind blew to the east.

Chapter 5

Hell's Factories

An important day dawned on 14 October. Hitler ordered all operations on the Eastern Front to end, with the exception of those in the Caucasus and Stalingrad. The time had now come for Paulus to deliver the city to his master as he had been ordered to do six days earlier. Sixth Army's staff had worked up their plan for the third attack which was essentially a repeat of what had gone before but with greater intensity. The main blow was to be struck between the Barrikady and Tractor factories, the victim 37th Guards Division, the objective to split Sixty-Second Army and roll it up along the riverbank.

The Soviet dispositions placed 308th Rifle Division, blocking the approaches to the Barrikady and the northern section of the Red October factory, on the left flank of 37th Guards with 95th Rifle Division to their rear as a reserve. Covering the southern section of Red October and the eastern slopes of the Mamayev Kurgan was 284th Siberian Division, which connected with 13th Guards Division at the end of the line. On the right flank of 37th Guards, between the Mechetka and Orlovka rivers, lay 112th Rifle Division's position connecting with 124 Rifle Brigade in Spartanovka and Rynok. None of these formations was approaching full strength; indeed many had drafted in factory workers to make up the numbers or had assumed control of smaller units. Nor was the line as clear-cut as implied. Small unit actions were continual as each side strove to gain the most advantageous positions. The 'Fritzes' controlled the daylight hours, the 'Ivans' the darkness.

At 08.00 hrs on 14 October, 14th Panzer Division, once again with overwhelming air support, led the attack. The Luftwaffe, aware that the Russians kept their front line as near as possible to their enemy's, countered with precision bombing. The accuracy of this tactic was described by a Russian veteran as follows. 'The German bombing of the factories was absolutely devastating. Everything more than 100 metres from the front line was blasted to smithereens. It brought chaos to our lines.' But, wherever conditions permitted, the Soviet infantry had dug deep, narrow trenches with as much overhead cover as possible, both for protection and for camouflage. German accounts of the war in the USSR often pay tribute to the Russians' skill with camouflage, or *Maskirovka*, as the Red Army described such things. However, German air and fire power was not only directed at the poor *Frontovik* (Red Army front-line men) but also at the unit command posts. Soviet radio traffic was continually monitored to locate the sites of headquarters. The Russians were aware of this and kept radio usage to a minimum but the almost total destruction of land lines during the bombardment on 14 October gave them no option but to use radio. During the course of the day's fighting both 37th Guards and 308th Rifle divisions' HQs were precisely hit. Even Chuikov's bunker behind the Barrikady was hit repeatedly despite the protection of the Volga embankment.

Although the Soviets held the first attack at bay the Germans continued to probe for weak points. Finally at 11.30 hrs 14th Panzer, supported by 100th Jager and 389th Infantry divisions, broke through 37th Guards' position towards the Barrikady and Tractor factories. While 60th Motorized Division pinned 112th Rifle Division along the Mechetka River, 14th Panzer cut east, slicing off 124 Rifle Brigade in Spartanovka. As the day wore on, elements of 112th Rifle Division merged with 124 Rifle Brigade as others pulled back into the grounds of the Tractor factory to join 37th Guards. By the end of the day Spartanovka was isolated, the Germans were on the Volga bank and the Tractor factory was under attack from three sides. With night falling, the Sixth Army seemed within sight of victory, having advanced over 1500 metres, which in Stalingrad terms was a colossal achievement. Chuikov remained sanguine, however, firm in the belief that the major blow would fall in the direction of the Red October factory. Nevertheless he reinforced the Tractor factory with men and munitions as it was the only thing preventing Sixth Army from rolling up Sixty-Second Army's position.

The following day Paulus committed 305th Infantry Division, increasing the pressure on 37th Guards, while 16th Panzer and 60th Motorized divisions chipped away at the Spartanovka Pocket. However, the results that day were disappointing and that night Chuikov received reinforcements, a regiment from 138th Siberian Division.

When fighting resumed on 16 October the German advance along the riverbank was held up by a line of well-entrenched T-34s. Pausing to realign, the German infantry were caught in the open by rocket and artillery fire from the eastern shore of the Volga. Near the Barrikady, 308th Rifle Division's right flank began to give ground but the timely arrival of the remainder of 138th Siberian Division that night propped up Chuikov's right flank. Reduced to defending a handful of buildings in Spartanovka, 124 Rifle Brigade was denied permission to evacuate to one of the islands to its rear. The release of any German units at this time was potentially catastrophic, so 124 Rifle continued to tie down as many as it could.

The T-34 line, 84 Tank Brigade, was singled out for Luftwaffe attention on 17 October. The dust and confusion created by the bombing gave German infantry the opportunity to slip through the cordon and into the Barrikady where they encountered 308th Rifle Division.

With more than half of the Tractor factory in enemy hands Chuikov could not afford to lose the Barrikady as well. Once more he moved his HQ, this time to the riverbank behind the Red October factory. It was to be his final relocation.

The next day the Germans concentrated on the Barrikady, cutting it off from the Tractor factory and taking a section of riverbank by mid-afternoon. Slowly but surely Sixth Army was slicing its opponents into digestible chunks.

In an attempt to relieve the pressure on Sixty-Second Army, Rokossovsky's Don Front launched yet another diversionary attack on Paulus's left flank. Despite its failure to make any significant headway the operation drew Luftwaffe assets from the skies over Stalingrad and it was impossible for the Germans to release ground forces for the city operations. Unfortunately for Stalingrad's defenders, at 11.30 hrs on 18 October 193rd Rifle Division's right flank collapsed forcing the withdrawal of 308th Rifle Division to within 650m of the Volga, where the line steadied. The Tractor factory fell into German hands two days later as fighting in Spartanovka and Barrikady continued. The time gained by the defenders of the Tractor factory had allowed Chuikov to prepare defences behind that position against which the Germans made little progress.

Once again a Soviet attack on the Sixth Army's flank, this time aimed at Fourth Panzer Army to the south of the Tsaritsa River, prevented Paulus from bringing fresh men. Sixty-Fourth Army pinned Hoth's forces in place for a week until the beginning of November.

As Shumilov's Sixty-Fourth Army tied down Fourth Panzer Army the long-awaited attack on the Red October factory commenced on 23 October. A completely fresh unit, 79th Infantry Division, supported by several battalions of combat engineers specially trained in streetfighting techniques, attacked the Barrikady and Red October factories. After savage fighting the Barrikady fell and Landing Stage 62, named for the army it supplied, came within clear shot of the Germans. But now the battle was taking place in amongst the rubble thrown up by days of continuous bombardment. Bricks and mortar had been shredded and shredded again, girders and railway lines twisted grotesquely skywards and amongst this surreal landscape the wounded screamed. Against such a hellish backdrop it is a wonder how either defenders or attackers retained their sanity when the front lines were often a staircase or the thickness of a sagging wall.

Fresh Soviet troops, the 45th Rifle Division, joined with 193rd Rifle Division between the Barrikady and Red October factories frustrating German attempts to split Sixty-Second Army into three.

As his infantry somehow held off the German onslaught in a maze of offices, workshops and machine tools Chuikov's decision to transfer his heavy artillery began to bear yet more fruit. Time and again Sixth Army's concentration and assembly points were hit and the impending assaults were broken up. The Red Air Force too was growing in strength, ambition and confidence. Night raids were carried out against Luftwaffe bases out on the western steppe and combined strikes with the artillery made Sixth Army's immediate rear a less than quiet post. It was in these conditions that the activities of the Storm Groups were stepped up. Raiding into German positions became an almost nightly occupation depriving the *Landser* of their sleep and, more importantly, their sense of security. Every German felt he was under the barrel of a gun, to paraphrase Chuikov. Despite controlling ninety per cent of the city the Sixth Army had not, by the end of October, been able to extinguish the last few thousand square metres of resistance and the temperature was dropping rapidly.

During the October fighting the Germans developed their skill at night fighting. Men of the 60th Motorized Division observe their handiwork following a raid into Spartanovka.

Incredibly, a large number of children, generally orphaned, roamed the Stalingrad area. Some hundreds eked out an existence working for the armies of both sides. These three are pounding cereals for the commissary at Gumrak airfield to the west of Stalingrad.

Seen from the Russian lines, a flight of Stukas prepares for a precision bomb run on 14 October. 'As on a string of pearls, one plane followed the others within an interval of a few seconds, throwing the bombs on the oblong area divided amongst us,' according to a Soviet veteran.

The reality of urban warfare, up close and very personal. A three-man submachine group prepares to repel an attack in the factory area. Wearing rural patterned camouflage smocks was as practical as any other clothing, given that everything assumed a uniform dust shade from particle-filled air.

Ducking and weaving under the dubious cover of a petroleum wagon, a Soviet infantryman negotiates his way back through the marshalling yards in front of the Barrikady factory. The original caption hints that he may have been a sniper but the lack of a telescopic sight calls this into question.

A short-barrelled assault gun makes its way towards the Red October factory late in October. A crew member mans an externally mounted machine-gun to ward off any lurking Soviet troops carrying Molotov cocktails or anti-tank mines.

Part of a flamethrower team, this man waits to move forward during the October thrust. He is located near the Park of Sculptures, which had retained much of its greenery.

A 45mm anti-tank gun, one of the type rapidly brought into action at the gates of the Tracto factory on 14 October by men of the 112th Rifle Division Weighing in at 560kg, it was easily man-portable and highly manoeuvrable.

A Storm Group cuts along a sunken lane behind the blazing hulk of the Tractor factory. The lead men are clearing the way with PPSh submachine-guns and grenades while the rear figure waits to take his ROKS 2 flamethrower into action. With a range of 50 metres, it was lethal at close quarters.

Leaving the shelter of their trench, lightly equipped German infantry prepare to flush out pockets of resistance in the factory district. Although areas were declared secure, official pronouncements were often meaningless, as counter-infiltration work went on continually.

By his belt, a Red Army man.

Men of the 308th Rifle Division run to take up defensive positions and give covering fire to their comrades amongst the outer buildings of the Barrikady factory. All appear to be armed with the PPSh machine-gun, an ideal weapon for close combat but less than accurate over 50 metres. It fired pistol ammunition and was simpler to produce than a rifle.

Pilots of 588 Night Bomber Regiment stand in front of one of their Po-2 wood-and-canvas biplanes. Also known as the U-2, this machine carried a load of 6 x 50kg bombs. Known to the Germans as the Night Witches, several ladies of this unit became Heroes of the Soviet Union.

Katyusha rocket launchers being prepared for firing. The effects of such a mass of explosives landing could be devastating. The principle governing their use was fire and move. Officially termed Guards Mortars to maintain secrecy, their simple construction appealed to Soviet military technologists.

Katyusha rockets launching at night.

A Naval Infantry mortar team on Zaitsevski Island prepares to fire in support of the 124 Rifle Brigade cut off in Spartanovka. The 120mm mortar they are loading had a range of 5700m and fired a 16kg round.

Even as the fighting closed up on the factories work went on. The Soviet combat engineers used mobile barriers, such as the one being completed here, as the basis for barricades against German armour. The damage to the building can be seen to the rear.

From the Sixty-Second Crossing straight into action for these men. The thick smoke would suggest burning oil storage facilities which hindered the Luftwaffe's bombing runs. This crossing became untenable on 26 October when the Germans reached to within 400 metres of it. However, each division had taken the precaution of establishing their own river supply system, which now came into operation.

Chapter 6

Retribution

With the coming of winter Chuikov faced what he called 'war on two fronts': the Germans to his front, the frozen Volga to his rear. The freezing-over of the river was not a problem; it was the period when ice floes ran thick and fast, disrupting if not sinking his supply vessels and the bridges to Zaitsevski Island that concerned him. Naturally Paulus was aware of this and wished to exploit it. The fighting during the first week of November typified what the Sixth Army termed *Rattenkrieg* – 'the war of the rats' – small vicious actions that provoked equally vicious counteractions, all played out amongst the tunnels, sewers and ghostly walls and rooms of ruined buildings. This period was, however, the calm before the storm. Sixth Army was about to unleash what became its final effort to annihilate Sixty-Second Army.

Ironically it was on 11 November at 06.30 hrs that the Luftwaffe opened the attack in an attempt to clear a route to the Volga. Fighting erupted on the Mamayev Kurgan, around the Lazur Chemical works and its surrounding railway sidings, an area known to the Luftwaffe as the 'tennis racket' due to its shape when viewed from the air.

On the ground 305th Infantry Division, supported by the combat engineers, broke through to the Volga, cutting off 138th Rifle Division in what became known to the Soviets as 'Lyudnikov's Island' after the divisional commander. Sixty-Second Army was now split into three. Localized night actions restored part of the Soviet position, but renewed German attacks the next day pushed the line nearer to the river's edge. But it was Paulus's last throw of the dice. Casualties during October had reduced his fighting strength significantly and now he ordered the Panzer divisions to contribute their crews as infantry. Aghast, the panzer commanders protested at this waste of skilled men. However, the order stood. Over the course of the next five days the operation wound down. Sixth Army was fought out. With the days shortening, Luftwaffe support was reduced and a strange calm pervaded the city.

Had he but known it, Paulus was about to become victim of months of meticulous Soviet planning. With majestic irony 12 September, the day on which Paulus expressed his concerns about the condition of his flank cover, was the date on which Zhukov (Deputy Supreme Commander after Stalin) and Vasilevsky (Chief of the General Staff) suggested the encirclement of Sixth Army to Stalin. The overextension of Sixth Army's supply lines and the weakness of the two Romanian armies guarding Sixth Army's left and right flanks, Third and Fourth armies respectively, provided the opportunity, and enlarged Soviet fronts would provide the means. One armoured pincer would thrust through Third Romanian Army, followed by another through Fourth Romanian Army. The pincers would meet at Kalach where Sixth Army's railway supply line crossed the Don River. The distances travelled by each pincer were 128km and 97km from the north and south respectively. Having isolated Sixth Army, part of the encircling forces would turn inwards to contain Paulus and part would face outwards along the Chir River to engage the anticipated relief effort. Zhukov explained that the build-up for the northern thrust would take place in the Serafimovich and Kletskaya bridgeheads. The reason for operating so far from the rear of Sixth Army was to deny it the opportunity to disengage its armoured divisions to break up the operation. A timescale of some seven weeks was allowed to put all the pieces in place for what was now codenamed Operation Uranus under the overall control of General Vasilevsky.

To facilitate the offensive South-Western Front was resurrected under the command of General Vatutin.

South-Western Front was to be built up under an intense blanket of security, deception and camouflage – a classic *Maskirovka*. The dates for the start of Operation Uranus were 9 and 10 November for north and south pincers respectively, the difference in time relating to the distance to be covered by each thrust.

Uranus was one of two offensives planned for the winter of 1942; the other was Operation Mars directed against Army Group Centre. Both operations were designed to be expanded in the wake of success.

Although the Romanians had an inkling of preparations being made on their armies' fronts and had been promised reinforcements, including much-needed heavy anti-tank guns, German military intelligence analysts were convinced that the major Soviet winter offensive would be directed at Army Group Centre. Furthermore they did not believe the Russians were capable of conducting two offensives simultaneously and that if an attack were launched in the south it would be later in the year or similar in scope to those mounted during recent months on the flanks of Sixth Army.

The concentration of forces at either end of the zone of operations was an immense logistical exercise. As well as moving in the troops and their equipment it was decided on 14 October to evacuate all civilians from within a 20km zone leading into the assembly areas. This was to include the non-essential civilian personnel remaining in Stalingrad. All empty villages were to be fortified as part of the *Maskirovka* aimed at convincing the Germans that the ongoing movements were purely defensive. Two days later Order 325 was issued from Moscow. It included tactical analysis and instructions for tank and mechanized forces down to company level. Part of the Uranus plan specified that armoured formations were to avoid getting tangled up in unnecessary actions that might delay the completion of the encirclement, both external and internal.

Approximately 1300 tanks and 700,000 men were gathered along the axis of Operation Uranus. However, this mammoth effort took longer than anticipated, therefore Zhukov requested, and was granted, a postponement of ten days until 19 November.

Finally all was reported as being ready. Sixty-Second Army had done all that was required of it, having drawn Sixth Army on and pinned it in Stalingrad. It was only as midnight passed on 18 November that Chuikov was informed of the counteroffensive. It was just in time – the Volga was freezing and the snow was coming down heavily.

Out on South-Western Front's steppe the code 'Send a messenger to pick up the fur gloves' was despatched. Translated it ordered, 'Infantry infantry attack begins at 08.50 hrs 19.11.42.'

Operation Uranus was about to begin.

During early November the weather alternated between frost and icy rain with monotonous regularity. This Soviet unit and its horse-drawn transport are making their way to an assembly point on the eastern bank of the Volga. By this time the Luftwaffe's ability to interfere with such daylight movements had diminished.

Men of 24th Panzer Division outside of their dugout show off their winter kit. Although the first heavy snow did not fall until 12 November the temperature had been well below freezing for more than a week. Their Panzer III shows no sign of a whitewash camouflage scheme.

A Storm Group makes a tentative approach to the next floor of an apartment block near the Red October factory. Not only did they have to worry about the Germans but the condition of the buildings themselves was often as hazardous. The Germans had developed their own version of the Storm Group, which carried out similar functions in a similar fashion.

Behind the lines the men of Sixth Army prepare for another winter in the snows of the USSR. Many units had put in orders for Christmas items such as trees, games and decorations. Others spent their time on preparing deep, insulated bunkers such as the one being constructed here by pioneers of 100th Jager Division.

The Germans destroyed any settlements to deny the Red Army or the civilian population shelter during the bitter winter. The Soviet attitude to civilians was not much better, as they regarded the majority of the civilians, particularly the Cossacks, as likely collaborators.

Carefully negotiating his way across the rubble-strewn floor, a Storm Group leader keeps his head low as he approaches a shell hole in the external wall of a manager's office in the Red October factory. The 37th Guards Division gained a fine reputation for the daring of its combat reconnaissance units.

The 138th Rifle Division counterattacks in the factory residential area. The Germans found the resilience and capacity of the Russians to mount even small, localized operations remarkable and were frequently caught off balance.

A German mortar prepares to fire a round at 284th Siberian Division on the Mamayev Kurgan. The 50mm mortar is poised at its most extreme elevation indicating the nearness of the target.

German infantry move past the hulk of a T-34, part of the line formed by 84 Tank Brigade in October. Each day that passed allowed the Russians time to strengthen their defences amongst the warren of bombed-out buildings. Moving anywhere for the Germans was an experience fraught with danger as Soviet snipers and scouts picked off the unwary. The taking of *tongues*, as purposely captured Germans were called, became a matter of competition between Soviet reconnaissance units.

A battalion gun prepares to fire from behind the Red October factory. Until the Stalingrad campaign the Russian artillery, although enjoying a high technical reputation, had put the preservation of its guns before other considerations. They were now seen to be there sharing the hardships of the infantry.

One of the classic images of Stalingrad, heavily laden German infantry scrambling over some ruins for the benefit of the press.

A *Nebelwerfer* is loaded prior to firing in support of Sixth Army's last major operation, which began on 11 November. Two regiments of such weapons, 2nd and 30th, fought at Stalingrad. Judging by its pristine condition this one has clearly just been wheeled out of one of the nearby shelters.

Holding his cap against the wind and shielding his field telephone, a gun commander takes fire orders relayed from a forward observation officer across the Volga. The artillery observers positioned in the rubble of the city shouldered a great responsibility as their accuracy of calculation controlled the fate of many of their comrades.

Soviet troops work to break on the ice on the banks of the Volga. The ice floes coming down the river posed an awful threat to the vessels keeping the supply line open. Coinciding with Paulus's last attempt to crush Sixty-Second Army, it was of grave concern to Chuikov. By 11 November the river was covered in an icy slush, *salo*, and a freezing wind blew continually. Such conditions affected not only Sixty-Second Army but also preparations for Operation Uranus to the north and south of the city.

As the frost, snow and rain alternately battered the southern USSR, Sixth Army's panzers required increased levels of maintenance. Many of the tanks and assault guns used during the November operation in Stalingrad had been removed to repair facilities nearer the Don River such as that of 16th Panzer, seen here at Kalach.

As November drew on, unit reports spelled out the deterioration of the men's morale. Leave was rare and the numbers falling ill increased. Much has been written on the stress of battle, the evidence of which is clear on the faces of these two men.

As Sixth Army's November assaults petered out Chuikov's strength had been reduced to roughly 47,000 men with nineteen tanks. In Spartanovka were some 1000, Lyudnikov's Island held about 500 and the remains of five infantry divisions, the strongest of which was 13th Guards with 1500. The army's total included not only the front-line strength but the artillerymen across the river, the supply services and other non-combatants.

A Russian *Hiwi* (*Hilfswillige*, or volunteer helper). These collaborators knew what was in store for them in the event of a Soviet victory. In many of Sixth Army's units they fought side by side with the Germans. Some were used to infiltrate Soviet lines to gather intelligence. If captured they were passed to the NKVD for interrogation prior to execution.

Armour and infantry move into their assembly area in the build-up to Operation Uranus. The overwhelming majority of movement was carried out at night. During the day men and machines were hidden in any available building to avoid the prying eyes of the Luftwaffe.

Stalin, pictured post war, had during the course of 1942 given his commanders a considerably greater deal of freedom to conduct operations than previously. Furthermore he had, on 9 October, reduced the power of the army's political officers relegating them to an advisory and educational role. The soldiers could now issue orders without looking to the *Politruk* (unit political commissar) for his approval.

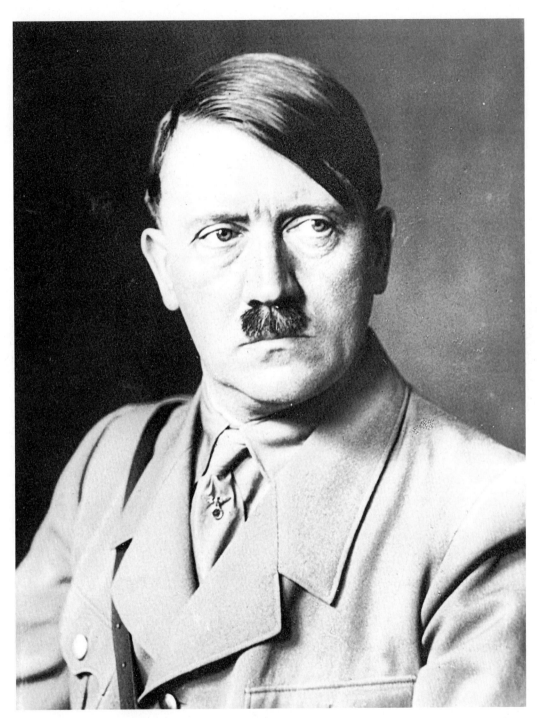

By contrast Hitler came to rely on his own inspiration rather than the advice of professionals when conducting operations. His decision not to permit Paulus to break out of the encirclement allowed Manstein the opportunity to hold open the escape route for Army Group A through Rostov. Whether both Sixth Army and Army Group A could have escaped destruction will remain a moot point.

Chapter 7

Rendezvous at Kalach

'Siren' was the codeword that ordered the Soviet artillery to begin its bombardment of Axis lines at 07.20 hrs Moscow time on 19 November. For eighty minutes a mixture of rockets, artillery and mortars belonging to the Don and South-Western fronts pounded their designated targets as the armour and infantry moved into their jump-off positions. Then, at 08.50 hrs Fifth Tank Army burst out of the Serafimovich Bridgehead hitting Third Romanian Army's left flank at its junction with Eighth Italian Army. Protection from intervention by the Italians was provided by First Guards Army. Despite holding off two Soviet attacks the Romanians' line was, by midday, pierced. As the mist which had blanketed the battlefield lifted, the Red Air Force's Second, Sixteenth and Seventeenth Air armies began to fly ground support missions. Don Front's Twenty-Fourth and Sixty-Sixth armies advanced on Vatutin's left flank.

Sixth Army's HQ heard nothing of the Soviet attack until mid-morning but later in the day news began to arrive of a major breakthrough. Army Group B's HQ, believing the Soviet attack from the Don Front was the main one, as had happened before, ordered 16th Panzer Division and IIL Panzer Corps to provide support. However, when it became apparent that the Romanians were giving way, IIL Panzer Corps was diverted to support 1st Armoured Division. The IIL Panzer Corps was, on paper, a powerful unit but in reality it disposed of just 100 serviceable tanks. The Romanian 1st Armoured Division was equipped with obsolete Skodas that were no match for T-34s. Communications with the Romanians broke down. Furthermore some thirty per cent of IIL Panzer Corps' tanks failed to start due to mice eating the wiring systems.

At 22.00 hrs Weichs ordered Paulus to break off operations in Stalingrad, 'with the objective of moving forces to cover the rear flank of Sixth Army and secure lines of communications.' During the early hours of 20 November the T-34s of XXVI Tank Corps hit the Skodas of 1st Romanian Armoured Division and cut them to pieces. Attempting to support the Romanians, 22nd Panzer Division failed and withdrew. The Soviets, now freed from distractions, continued on their way to Kalach. Sixth Army meanwhile was ordered to send its armoured and motorized divisions westwards but this proved problematic, as crews had been assigned infantry roles, fuel was scarce and, due to Chuikov's pinning attacks, they had difficulty disengaging from combat. Consequently many of these units did not get under way until after midnight on 21 November and by then the Soviet pincer to the south of the city had begun to cut into Fourth Romanian Army.

Stalingrad Front's barrage commenced at 10.00 hrs on 20 November, a couple of hours behind schedule due to thick fog. This flank presented less resistance and the breakthrough came after only two hours of fighting. However, Fifty-Seventh Army's tanks ran into 29th Motorized Division, which held up the Soviet advance until ordered to take up position on the Chir River just as Hoth's Fourth Panzer Army HQ withdrew westwards. Fourth Romanian Army was now on its own, but blizzards and an overcautious field commander slowed the Soviet advance.

At his HQ at Golubinsky on the Don, Paulus watched as the northern flank of Sixth Army was inexorably driven back towards Stalingrad by Rokossovsky's Don Front and both Romanian armies began to collapse. The Romanians had done the best they could but, with little or no armoured support and fewer anti-tank weapons, they no longer presented a cohesive front to north or south, merely pockets of stubborn resistance. As 21 November drew on, Soviet tanks were reported to be close by and Paulus relocated his HQ to Gumrak airfield roughly 13km west of Stalingrad. The progress of the northern Soviet armoured thrust towards Kalach was gaining momentum while cavalry were exploiting holes in XI Corps' line north of the city forcing it to fall back towards the Don River. Stalingrad Front's advance had increased its pace and all Soviet eyes now focussed on the bridge at Kalach.

Taken by surprise, on 22 November the Germans at Kalach lost the bridge to XXVI Tank Corps, who on the following day connected with troops from Stalingrad Front's IV Tank Corps 15km to the east.

Sixth Army's announcement to Army Group B's HQ that it was encircled noted, 'little fuel left. Ammunition is short, provisions will last for six days […] request freedom of action.' It was on 23 November that Hitler declared Stalingrad a Fortress (Festung). As he did so, XI Corps, north of the fortress, was conducting a withdrawal, fighting off Soviet attacks from three sides. The force included numerous Romanian stragglers. As XI Corps approached the Don River crossing points many units began to lose cohesion as the desire to survive took precedence over discipline. The wounded were abandoned as the fuel for ambulances was distributed to tanks or artillery tractors. As their cavalry harried the Germans, Soviet infantry crossed the Don on 25 November, as by then it had frozen solid. The next day the last bridge was blown and Sixth Army was cut off, with its rear units scurrying for the city, between the Volga and the Don rivers. As the South-Western, Stalingrad and Don fronts developed their inner and outer perimeters the NKVD followed in their wake to flush out collaborators and deserters from the liberated villages and POW camps.

Hitler had not been idle. On 20 November he had appointed Field Marshal Manstein commander of the newly created Army Group Don, which included the two shattered Romanian armies, Sixth Army and Fourth Panzer Army. Army Group Don's purpose was to stabilize the front in southern Russia and relieve the Kessel (surrounded area) that Sixth Army occupied. Three days later Paulus was ordered to 'adopt hedgehog (all round) defence, present Volga line and northern front to be held at all costs.' The message ended optimistically, 'supplies coming by air.' In fact part of the fortress's garrison had already attempted, unilaterally, to provoke a breakout but had failed. Livid, Hitler had split the command structure in Stalingrad, wrongly blaming Paulus for the botched attempt. Manstein arranged for Paulus to be reinstated almost immediately. Now Sixth Army fell to the task of organizing its hedgehog position in what became known as the 'fortress without a roof'.

Twenty-two divisions, numbering almost 250,000 men, were trapped inside the pocket, which measured 56km by 40km with a perimeter of some 130km. Seven Soviet armies (a Soviet army equated to a German corps), the entirety of Stalingrad and Don fronts including Twenty-First Army from South-Western Front and Sixty-Second Army itself held the line of inner encirclement. The outer perimeter ran for 322km along the courses of the Chir, Don and Aksay rivers between 30 and 50km to the west. Fourth Panzer Army had retained a bridgehead over the Chir at Kotelnikovo and out on the steppe to the south-east 16th Motorized Division patrolled the bleak expanse between Army Group Don and Army Group A down in the Caucasus.

South-Western Front was also consolidating its position and dealing with the critical need for food, fuel and ammunition. As this time-consuming and difficult task was being carried out Vasilevsky turned his attention to the expansion plans for Uranus – Operation Saturn, which was even more far-reaching in ambition and distance. South-West, with Voronezh Front on its right flank, would crush Eighth Italian Army then drive south-westwards to take Rostov on Don at the end of the Sea of Azov. This operation would cut off Army Group A in the Caucasus along with Army Group Don. Stalin gave his permission for Saturn to go ahead on 26 November, allowing Vasilevsky until 10 December to redeploy and reinforce his attacking groups, sometimes known as Shock Armies. However, the Germans had plans of their own and Sixth Army would not simply collapse of its own accord. Having discussed the situation with Zhukov, Stalin instructed Vasilevsky to concentrate on the Stalingrad Fortress as Zhukov believed that Manstein was planning to break through and relieve Paulus. Indeed he was: planning was in hand for Operation Winter Storm, the offensive to turn the Soviet tide and break into the *Kessel*.

Clad in their camouflage coveralls, Soviet infantry jump from their transport to engage enemy infantry on the first day of Operation Uranus. A lack of lorries or armoured personnel carriers forced the Soviets to move supporting infantry in this manner. Such specialist troops were known as 'tank desant men'. Sitting targets until they dismounted, their casualties were heavy.

Model 1941 T-34/76s undercover blend well into the mixed terrain. One of the reasons for the postponement of Uranus was a lack of winter lubricants. Refuelling en route to Kalach was problematic and was carried out to the detriment of food and transport for the wounded. The aerial indicates a unit commander's vehicle.

A 152mm gun prepares to fire in support of South-Western Front's attack on 19 November. With a range of 25km such pieces were capable of firing one 49kg shell every two minutes. To deploy these and other heavy guns the artillery commanders referred to manuals from the First World War.

A Skoda 38 of 16th or 22nd Panzer division prepares to move off into the misty steppe on 19 November. It was a more modern tank than the Skoda 35 used by the Romanians. With fewer bogies than the 35 it was less likely to get clogged with snow, mud and slush.

Soviet troops from both north and south meet up and listen to a speech from a senior officer or *Politruk*. The majority of Soviet infantry were not yet issued with camouflage outfits. The meeting took place just east of Kalach in the hamlet of Sovetsky.

As the Soviet pincers closed in, all manner of German units headed for the apparent safety of Stalingrad. Often with little warning they left snug quarters for the open steppe. Here one such group arrives at Gumrak airfield on 27 November with others following in the distance.

Captured German tanks, such as this Panzer III, enabled the capture of Kalach during the early morning of 22 November. Pretending to be a German unit, men of 19 Tank Brigade drove the captured vehicles up to the western end of the bridge and before the German garrison could recover from its surprise, took the bridge and prevented its destruction. The town of Kalach on the eastern bank, filled with Romanian stragglers, fell later in the day.

If there was time, retreating German forces destroyed any buildings they vacated simply to deny shelter to the Soviets. However, despite their efforts, several supply dumps were captured intact and allowed the Soviets to replenish their supplies of food and fuel. On occasion Soviet infantry were reported to have eaten themselves to death or died drinking apparently alcoholic liquids.

A section of T-60 tanks transports troops across an unfrozen stream in late November. The changeable nature of the weather often upset the Soviet timetable. Although conditions were gradually deteriorating, periods of mild, rainy weather turned the ground to a muddy slush which usually froze again at night sealing tracked vehicles into the ground.

Death in the open. These German anti-aircraft gunners were caught up in the increasingly chaotic retreat of XI Corps north of Stalingrad. Scratch units were put together to cover the approaches to the Don at Luchinsky to cover the 44th Infantry Division crossing. However, not all of them reached safety before the bridge was blown.

Romanian and German POWs wait for orders to move down to the barges that will transport them across to the eastern bank of the Volga. Obviously cold and demoralized, many of the Romanians opted to join the Soviet-sponsored Tudor Vladimirescu Division during the following year. For the Germans there was no alternative but imprisonment.

Kalmyk cavalry head for the Don crossings. Members of two squadrons attached to 16th Panzer Division, the Kalmyks were vehemently anti-communist. Mounted on sturdy ponies, which they were famous for breeding, such men would have received scant mercy if captured. Their role was that of mounted scouts. They fought against Soviet cavalry units along the flanks of XI Corps.

The supply airlift to Stalingrad began on 23 November but within two days over thirty transport aircraft had been lost and bombers were pressed into service, as shown here. From the beginning it was obvious that the Luftwaffe had insufficient planes to carry the minimum estimate of 300 tons per day to keep Sixth Army going. German nurses were amongst the first personnel evacuated.

Men of South-Western Front's infantry divisions charge for the camera. By late November the troops of Sixty-Second Army had received winter clothing. But this still was not the case out on the steppe.

A T-34 bounces across muddy ground on one of the more clement days.

The ubiquitous Fieseler *Storch* (Stork). Produced in its thousands, the Stork was used to transport senior officers, carry out reconnaissance missions and to evacuate the wounded. Its ability to land and take off with under 75 metres of runway made it invaluable in the compacted air space over Stalingrad, as did its low stalling speed of 40kmph, which allowed it almost to hover.

Hastily entrenched, a German 50mm mortar team makes ready to fire. As the Soviet encirclement drew nearer to Stalingrad many former Soviet defence positions were refurbished and put to use by the Axis troops.

Soviet cavalry, not Cossacks, who slung their carbines over their right shoulders, keep watch for Axis stragglers. The Red Army maintained cavalry divisions well into the 1950s. The steppe ponies were capable of finding fodder under the most trying of conditions and were renowned for their stamina.

Assault guns prepare to move out for their start lines as Army Group Don gears up for Operation Winter Storm.

Chapter 8

Defeat on the Myshkova River

As Stavka prepared for Operation Saturn, so Manstein prepared for Winter Storm. Army Group Don was given 336th Infantry Division, 7th and 15th Luftwaffe divisions (infantry) and 11th Panzer Division with 6th and 23rd Panzer divisions en route. The only operation that Hitler was agreeable to would open and maintain a supply corridor to Stalingrad. Manstein lacked the resources to accomplish this as well as stabilize the front and cover Army Group A's rear. Meanwhile Vasilevsky, under the illusion that Sixth Army numbered less than 100,000 men, ordered Stalingrad and Don fronts to reduce the pocket by attacking its northern sector and link up at Gumrak. Stalingrad Front led off on 2 December and Don Front joined the fray two days later. Both attacks ran into a well-organized defensive system that responded well to changes of attack lane. The rapidity with which Paulus shuffled his reserves showed that there were more men and fighting capacity left in Sixth Army than anticipated. After suffering heavy losses Vasilevsky called a halt. Stalin supported this decision and reinforced Vasilevsky with the nine divisions of Second Guards Army. With this additional support Rokossovsky was instructed to draw up plans for the destruction of Sixth Army in an offensive to be called Operation *Koltso* (Ring). As Stalin considered the draft of *Koltso* rumours reached Vasilevsky of Manstein's build-up on the Chir River and at Kotelnikovo. During the first week of December Fifth Tank Army crossed the frozen Chir straight into the teeth of 11th Panzer Division. The German line held, driving back the Soviet attack but it forced Manstein to modify his plans and reduce his efforts to a single thrust towards Stalingrad from the Kotelnikovo rail and bridgehead. Initially he had anticipated a double attack with a second pincer crossing the Chir. Identifying Fifty-First Army as Stalingrad Front's weak link, Manstein launched his panzers on 12 December. Although the distance from Kotelnikovo to the *Kessel* was longer the terrain was easier despite the Aksay and Myshkova rivers running directly across the route. Both 6th and 23rd Panzer divisions made speedy progress into Fifty-First Army's position. However, the decision whether or not to allow Sixth Army to break out remained in the hands of the Fuhrer. A codeword, Thunderclap, would grant Paulus permission to leave the Volga. Vasilevsky had to assume that Paulus would be allowed to break out but he ordered Second Guards Army to move the 190km to support Stalingrad Front and block Manstein's advance.

General Voronov now took charge of Operation Saturn and on 14 December Operation *Koltso* was postponed. The forces comprising the inner encirclement, particularly Fifty-Seventh and Sixty-Fourth armies to the south, were told to deny Paulus any regrouping opportunities and to 'nip off any attempt to break out of the ring.' By 17 December 6th and 23rd Panzer divisions had crossed the Aksay, having spent three days breaking down the resistance of IV Mechanized Corps and XIII Tank Corps. On the same day 17th Panzer Division arrived and the weather improved allowing Richthofen to provide air cover. Even so, the panzers could not do more than gain a tiny foothold on the Soviet bank on the Myshkova River.

Finally, on 18 December, leading elements of Second Guards Army began to arrive and expand into the Myshkova line flanked to their left by Fifty-First Army and to their right by Fifth Shock Army along the Chir where it was to pin IIL Panzer Corps as part of Stavka's next offensive, which became known as Little Saturn. The decision to reduce the scope of Saturn had been taken on 12 December when Second Guards Army was transferred. Rostov was no longer the target but Army Group Don's rear and Eighth Italian Army were still in the Soviet's sights.

The first stage was to force the Germans out of their bridgeheads on the Chir–Don confluence at Niznhe Chirskaya and maintain the pressure so that IIL Panzer Corps could not move.

The attack on the Italians began at 08.00 hrs on 16 December but it immediately ran into problems, as did the attack along the Chir. But renewed pressure over the next two days by Soviet Sixth Army and First Guards Army ripped a 48km gap in the Italian line. Furthermore the line along the Chir began to give way. On 19 December First and Third Guards armies met up, having encircled much of Italian Eighth Army. With the majority of its armoured forces tied up by Operation Winter Storm there was little or nothing that could be sent north to help Gariboldi's men as they tried to fight their way westwards. Once again T-34s raced south across the steppe with logistical objectives in mind – the airfields at Tatinskaya and Morozovsk. These two were the main bases for the air bridge in to the *Kessel* but both were also vital rail junctions for Army Group Don. By 23 December XXIV Tank Corps was 193km from its start point and 24 hours later it overran Tatinskaya. However, it was recaptured five days later and Morozovsk did not fall.

As the forces engaged in Little Saturn fought their way to their objectives and Winter Storm was halted on the Myshkova, the moment to announce Thunderclap passed.

It is highly unlikely that Sixth Army could have achieved anything more than a speedier demise had it attempted to break out to the south-west. Reduced to some seventy operational tanks, with scarcely enough fuel for more than 20km and with his draught horses either eaten or so undernourished they could barely support themselves, Paulus's mobility was virtually nil. Now his only slim hope lay with the Luftwaffe improving its performance, and the capacity of his men to hold out.

The Soviets' ability to rapidly respond to changing circumstances and Stalin's increased trust in his officer corps had paid remarkable dividends. With Army Group Don's situation becoming increasingly more perilous the fate of Army Group A in the Caucasus hung in the balance.

At 08.00 hrs on 24 December Stalingrad Front counterattacked along the Myshkova River and within three days it had pushed the Germans back beyond the start line of Winter Storm. Hitler now bowed to the inevitable: with little or nothing in the way of the Soviet advance Rostov was threatened and should it fall Army Group A was lost. Therefore on 28 December he ordered it to withdraw from the Caucasus and granted Manstein permission to establish a defence line 240km west of Stalingrad.

Within his perimeter Paulus had an incomplete picture of events outside. For Chuikov, however, the situation was infinitely better. On 16 December the Volga froze allowing supplies to cross in greater and greater quantities at a variety of less vulnerable points. Sixth Army's increasing shell shortage had reduced supply interception bombardments to a minimum, making it possible for Sixty-Second Army to wallow in a relative mountain of luxuries. The Red Air Force now dominated the skies over the city as the Luftwaffe had concentrated its resources on protecting the transport flights or covering Army Group Don. But for the ordinary soldiers life was degenerating into a continually stressful struggle to keep warm, safe and somehow hopeful. All supplies were now the responsibility of a central depot and many units had prepared good, solid defensive systems with decent, warm bunkers. But when the fact of Manstein's failure leaked out morale began to fall. Nevertheless the preparations for Christmas proceeded apace, as did skywatching to see how many transports arrived at Pitomnik or Gumrak airfields. Some patrolling was carried out and prisoners were taken by both sides. Those Germans lucky enough to be wounded and given the correct documentation to be airlifted out faced a gruelling journey to the airfield and then a wait in an overcrowded field hospital. Frostbite victims were not permitted to be evacuated as such an injury could have been self-inflicted.

Christmas services were held but the season of goodwill was broken by a Soviet attack on 16th Panzer Division's sector to the north-east of the pocket. It was part of pattern that had developed of attacks timed for dawn or dusk following mortar and artillery preparation. Such events were more of a minor irritation as Soviet resources were being husbanded for Rokossovsky's postponed Operation *Koltso*.

Pictured here during the siege of Sevastopol earlier in 1942, Manstein was well aware that the men of Sixth Army were too weak to survive the rigours of a fighting withdrawal across the open steppe. A master of mobile, defensive warfare, Manstein was to deliver a firm rebuff to the Soviets at Kharkov during February and March 1943.

A Panzer IV of 23rd Panzer Division during Operation Winter Storm at a refuelling stop on 18 December. By that date the combined destroyed and captured total for 23rd and 17th Panzer divisions was 167 Soviet tanks. The long 75mm gun shown here was particularly effective against the T-34. Spare track sections have been welded to the front to provide enhanced protection.

Second Guards Army tanks and infantry travelled together to reach the Myshkova River. Carrying up to twenty infantrymen, armoured vehicles were used in place of lorries. Lucky the man with a place near the exhausts or engines, as the wind chill factor was considerable. However, speed was of the essence and the comfort of the men was a secondary consideration.

Fighting in Stalingrad continued as operations Winter Storm and Little Saturn roared back and forth across the steppe. Here a machine-gun team of Rodimtsev's 13th Guards Division provides covering fire during the recapture of German strongpoints. Buildings such as the L Shaped House, the House of Specialists and the House of Railway workers along the Volga had all been heavily fortified. Soviet artillery was sometimes used at point-blank range to blast a way in.

The arrival of 6th Panzer Division from France was a welcome addition to Manstein's force. Its arrival at Kotelnikovo was just in time to prevent its capture. On 3 December it inflicted heavy casualties on the cavalry of IV Cavalry Corps near Pakhlebin. Still sporting their grey western European colours two Sd.Kfz 250 command vehicles carry senior officers on a reconnaissance mission.

Luftwaffe ground crew manhandle a parachute supply canister to a Ju-52 transport plane at Morozovsk airfield. Sixth Army's request that white parachutes be dyed red was ignored and the majority simply disappeared or fell into Soviet hands. Only once, during the first week of December, did the Luftwaffe manage to reach its daily target of 300 tons. Sixth Army was by then reducing its rations dramatically. The Soviet POWs at the camp near this airfield received little or nothing and died in their hundreds.

A 20mm anti-aircraft gun, under precarious shelter, covers the rear of Field Police at Pitomnik airfield. The Field Police had the unenviable task of controlling the crowds of wounded and others waiting to be airlifted out. When an aircraft arrived a mob would surge forward in an attempt to get a place. Such sights rattled the nerves of the younger aircrew, accustomed as they were to a more disciplined life behind the lines. Their descriptions of events fuelled the rumours of impending disaster that gradually spread back to Germany.

A remarkable image, taken from a German POW, showing a German foraging party moving along a civilian-inhabited *balka* searching for food. Despite the evacuations and deportations thousands of civilians still existed in the city. Digging into the sides of *balkas* was a common way of creating shelter. As German authority waned such areas became unsafe for Germans unless in groups and armed. Such civilian encampments often traded food and alcohol with the occupying forces.

Soviet cavalry bear down on Italians caught in the open. Although most of the Eighth Army was pushed westwards or encircled, the Alpine Corps on the left flank managed to withdraw in good order and put themselves under the command of the Second Hungarian Army, which held the line south of Voronezh. The Hungarians were convinced that they were a Soviet target but were unable to discern any details due to the efficiency of the *Maskirovka*.

Seen from the ground a Ju-52 approaches Pitomnik airfield inside Sixth Army's perimeter. There were three airfields within the *Kessel*; the others were Gumrak and Stalingrad itself. The latter was incapable of coping with transport aircraft. Fuel and ammunition were the priority cargoes but with extra fuel for the flight the payload was reduced to a little less than 2 tons.

Men of 284th Rifle Division scurry along their communications trench on the Mamayev Kurgan. The ground is clearly iron-hard. Exploding rounds on such surface ripped up razor-sharp shards of ice to add to the effects of the shrapnel. The winter winds also affected mortar bombs, which fell short of their targets. The Mamayev had developed into a potent symbol of the city's defence, and control of its commanding height was essential.

The face of this *Kesselhund* (hound) tells much of the condition of the city's defenders during the last days of 1942. Many men were outraged to hear German State Radio broadcast a choir 'from Stalingrad' singing Silent Night. The mood of the men fluctuated wildly between euphoria at rumours of a second relief expedition and depression when no transports flew in. Such doubts and fears were kept from their families in letters home.

A Soviet attack on a village out on the steppe on New Year's Day 1943. The day was also marked by a Soviet barrage and an attack in Spartanovka involving three companies that repelled by machine-gun and mortar fire. When it was over a German NCO recorded, 'We were so weak and exhausted and there were so many dead lying around in the open frozen stiff, that we could not even bury our own comrades.' Such sights were no longer uncommon as men could not physically dig in rock-hard ground.

Artillery observers at work in the rubble of one of the city's apartment blocks. The neat appearance of the men is not posed. Soviet veterans remember that, 'Nearly every day we shave; the Germans are all unshaved and untidy. Every soldier goes to the bath-house (across the Volga) and also gets a new set of underwear. But the Germans – they don't wash and they don't shave, and it makes a big difference.'

Watching and waiting. A German officer, well-dressed for the conditions, spots for an artillery unit. By the middle of December every round counted. Batteries were limited to 1.5 shells per day. The airlift on 26 December managed to provide 10 tons of sweets but no shells. With the weight of one round of 105mm ammunition weighing 28kg a Ju-86, the other transport plane, could only carry thirty-five — less than five minutes' firing.

Warmly clad Soviet cavalry ride past an abandoned German 37mm anti-tank gun during Little Saturn. As Little Saturn proved so successful Vatutin was granted permission by Moscow on 19 December to upgrade it to the original Saturn's specifications. Soviet tactical and strategic flexibility were notable at this time but Stalin's impatience was to cost the Red Army dear during Operation Mars.

When Tatinskaya airfield was recaptured by the Germans in late December they found the remains of over 70 transport aircraft, mainly Ju-52s, as seen here. The Soviets had caught nearly 200 aircraft in the process of escaping. The XXIV Tank Corps had a field day shooting them up as they taxied across the snow. The destruction of aircraft at Tatinskaya reduced the Luftwaffe's transport capacity by almost ten per cent.

An officer of 23rd Panzer Division keeps watch from the turret of his Panzer III. By 26 December 17th and 23rd Panzer divisions had been reduced to just twenty-three operational tanks. However, as they withdrew to a more defensible line more were brought into operation. Contrary to some claims Tiger tanks did not take part in Operation Winter Storm. Heavy Panzer Battalion 503, a Tiger unit, was involved in the defence of Rostov during the early weeks of 1943.

Every day, circumstances permitting, the Red Army issued its men with 100 grams of vodka. Known as 'the 100 grams', it was the equivalent of a quarter of a pint and was regarded as the highlight of the day. When casualties were high the individual ration was proportionately greater. As one man drinks from a German mess tin, a highly prized trophy, another looks on enviously waiting for his share.

Chapter 9

Victory on the Volga

Operation *Koltso* (Ring) was originally designed as an offensive in three parts that would break the Stalingrad pocket into easily manageable chunks. Initially Don Front would destroy 44th, 76th, 376th and 384th Infantry divisions to the north-west of the Rossosh River out on the steppe.

Secondly Sixty-Fourth Army would attack in the direction of Voroporovo cutting off the nose of the pocket's western salient towards its tip at Marianovka, then it would meet up with Don Front heading south-eastwards.

Finally with units of both Don and Stalingrad fronts united they would head east towards the Volga, fragmenting the Germans and Romanians as they retreated. Stalin's rider to his plan was that parts one and two should be conducted simultaneously. Postponed by Operation Winter Storm, *Koltso* was reactivated at the end of December as Army Group Don withdrew to protect the rear of Army Group A as it retired from the Caucasus. Interestingly, Red Army Intelligence put the number of troops trapped in Stalingrad at 86,000.

In the light of changes in the situation around Stalingrad, Voronov and Rokossovsky modified the original plan. To simplify command and control Stavka decided that the whole operation should come under the control of Rokossovsky's Don Front. The Stalingrad Front would be disbanded on 1 January 1943 and Yeremenko was sent to take command of the newly created Southern Front, an altogether larger force tasked with advancing on Rostov to cut off Army Group A.

Rokossovsky and Voronov's new draft was amended on 28 December and in this form Operation *Koltso* was to go ahead.

Fifty-Seventh Army would mount a major attack from the south and link up Twenty-First and Sixty-Fifth armies moving from the west through the 'nose'. The role of Sixty-Sixth Army, attacking from the north, was increased to cut off the factory district. Sixty-Fourth and Sixty-Second armies were to, as Rokossovsky put it, 'pin down as many enemy forces as possible and deny him the opportunity of manoeuvring.' Reinforcements were to be despatched to increase Don Front's infantry strength. Now it had expanded to 47 divisions, 5610 guns and mortars and 169 tanks – roughly 218, 000 men with support from 300 aircraft of Sixteenth Air Army. The start date was set for 6 January and when the first phase was completed, theoretically after six days, Rokossovsky would provide a more detailed proposal for part two.

However, reinforcing Don Front took longer than anticipated and Voronov was forced to request a delay. Stalin, clearly mellowing with the successes of his armies, granted another four days but insisted that Paulus be given the opportunity to surrender. Continually checking with Stalin, Voronov prepared a document that was translated by German communist exiles posted to Stalingrad for propaganda and intelligence work.

While Voronov agonized over the words and procedures, Rokossovsky's men moved into the line and the airlift attempted to keep the bodies and souls of Sixth Army together. As the Soviets' advance to the west continued the Luftwaffe was forced to relocate its transport airfields further from Stalingrad. Consequently the attrition rates of aircraft, ground crew and pilots cut the number of missions that were flown, and therefore the tonnage that reached Paulus declined sharply. Voronov's capitulation terms were rejected out of hand on 9 January and that night the bread ration in the *Kessel* was cut to 75 grams. Sustained by that and the odd bowl of horsemeat soup, Sixth Army's mixed bag of veterans, rear echelon men and Soviet collaborators waited for the inevitable.

At 08.05 hrs Moscow time Don Front's artillery let rip. Fifty-five minutes later the engines of the T-34s and the Soviet battle cry '*Urrah*' were heard all along the line as Sixty-Fifth Army, following a creeping barrage and accompanied by ground-attack aircraft went into the attack.

It was the moment that Chuikov's Sixty-Second Army had been waiting for. 'Bulletproof Batyuk', as his men affectionately called him, led his 284th Siberian Rifle Division surging once again up the slopes of the Mamayev Kurgan and on 11 January they planted the Red Flag on the summit where the whole city could see it. So reduced was Batyuk's command that it fought on as several large Storm Groups, and not a division. That other scene of carnage and brutality, the Red October factory, was also recaptured the same day. Charging from their positions within 250 metres of the Volga, 45th Rifle Division burst through the lines of 79th Infantry Division, which they faced for weeks across the factory's grounds.

As Sixty-Fifth Army battered its way into Sixth Army's perimeter it was supported to left and right by Twenty-Fourth and Twenty-First armies respectively. Rokossovsky received a stream of information that German forces west of the Rossosh River were in total disarray and the Marianovka Salient had gone. German 44th Infantry, 29th Motorized and 376th Infantry divisions were all but destroyed although 3rd Motorized Division was pulling back in relatively good order. The Germans scattered across the steppe, all headed for the perceived sanctuary of the city itself. Just west of Rynok the last serviceable tanks of 16th Panzer Division fought off an attack by T-34s. At the same time Sixty-Fourth Army, to the south, struck at 297th Infantry Division. During the initial barrage a Romanian battalion broke, leaving a gap that was plugged with considerable difficulty. Shocked at the strength of German resistance, Rokossovsky paused to regroup on 13 January. Soviet casualties for the first three days of *Koltso* amounted to 26,000 men and over eighty-five tanks.

The next phase of *Koltso* was led by Twenty-First Army. During the next ten days the main airfields fell amidst scenes of indescribable horror and chaos at the attached field hospitals. Five more of Sixth Army's divisions lost all fighting value and by this time any meaningful order of battle or defensive scheme was futile. Then, in the early hours of 26 January Twenty-First and Sixty-Fifth armies made contact with 13th Guards Division in the worker's settlement north of the Mamayev Kurgan. Sixth Army was split in two. When Gumrak fell Paulus made his final HQ relocation to the cellars of the ruined Univermag department store in the city centre, over which flew a tattered Nazi banner.

Paulus and his staff were trapped in the southern pocket with a few healthy troops to defend them, and thousands of stragglers and wounded. The northern pocket was under the command of General Strecker, who was determined to fight to the last man and the last bullet. Some men banded together and tried to escape through the confusion of the Soviet advance but none are known to have succeeded. On 31 January Paulus was promoted to the rank of Field Marshal, not in recognition of his services but in the hope that he would commit suicide rather than besmirch his honour and that of Germany by surrendering – an event which no German Field Marshal had ever allowed himself to survive. Paulus's mental and physical condition were such that his chief of staff had effectively taken command. He was hell-bent on obeying the Fuhrer's order sent on 9 January that Sixth Army must not surrender. But for the southern pocket there was to be no Wagnerian end to their suffering.

All around the Univermag department store men were surrendering in droves. At 07.45 on 31 January Sixth Army's successor unit in Taganrog received the message, 'We are surrendering' from Paulus. As the signal was transmitted to Manstein, Paulus was being led away to formally capitulate to Sixty-Fourth Army.

The fate of the northern pocket was different. Paulus refused to order Strecker to surrender, insisting that only Hitler himself could issue such a directive. Hitler had ordered Strecker to, 'resist to the last to tie down as much enemy strength as possible to facilitate operations on other fronts.' Recognition was thus given to the meaning of Sixth Army's sacrifice. Refusing permission to surrender to various unit commanders who visited him during the night of 1/2 February, Strecker gained Manstein another 24 hours. With Don Front's artillery ranged around the factory district the honour of conducting the final barrage was given to Chuikov. For the man whose army's motto was, 'there is no land across the Volga' it was appropriate that he oversaw his opponents' final hours of agony. Strecker's final signal ended, 'Long live Germany.' At 16.00 hrs on February 2 the last diehards surrendered. And as the columns of POWs made their way across the frozen Volga into captivity a private of the 45th Rifle Division wrote, 'Glorious Stalingrad is free.' It was a fitting tribute to the men of Chuikov's Sixty-Second Army.

Searching for deserters or malingerers became a full-time occupation for the Field Police as units decayed and were amalgamated. As well as the fighting men of the army divisions stragglers from the Organization Todt, the Luftwaffe, the Romanian Fourth Army and an unfortunate group of Italians looking for timber were also cut off in the city. It has been estimated that less than twenty per cent of the *Kessel's* 250,000 men were combat troops.

The stark reality of urban warfare is softened by the snow and the lack of human beings, dead or alive.

At the same time as *Koltso* was under way other offensives were liberating southern Russia and the Caucasus. The first of these, Operation *More* (Sea) pushed part of Army Group A into the Taman Peninsula and began on 4 January. Eight days later Voronezh Front began the elimination of Second Hungarian Army and on 16 January Operation *Gory* (Mountain) was launched to clear the remainder of Army Group A from the Caucasus. The T-34 seen here is firing at a Hungarian column.

The desolation following a tank battle out on the steppe. The hulks of armoured vehicles and the grotesquely frozen bodies of their crew litter the ground.

Two healthy men assist a comrade to an aid station. The situation for the wounded was dire. Lack of medical supplies, medicines and staff made any injury almost a death sentence. When the air bridge suspended operations almost all hope for such men was gone.

In a desperate attempt to increase the capacity of the airlift several of the Luftwaffe's largest bombers, the Fw 200 Condor, were drafted in early January. The Condor had a payload of 6 tons but, with the loss of Pitomnik and Gumrak airfields on 16 and 23 January respectively, its contribution was short-lived. Fighter and Stuka units flew off from each leaving Sixth Army with no air bridge or air cover. The situation was now obviously hopeless to the men left in the *Kessel*. Any dreams of flying out or airborne reinforcements were shattered.

The *Luftpost* into the *Kessel* ended early in January, but for Sixty-Second Army the mail always got through. A happy postman prepares to leave on his round from a shell hole on the Volga bank. Soviet intelligence made much use of captured letters recovered from crashed aircraft to judge the morale of the *Kessel*'s defenders. Indeed, broadcasting text from these letters did much to undermine the morale of the men and units concerned, particularly towards the end when the writers had become more pessimistic in their tone.

As the airlift tailed off, space on the planes was given to specialists. When it became clear that Sixth Army was not going to survive, a new 'Special Staff' under Field Marshal Milch was established at Taganrog to support Stalingrad. It was to this area that men such as those pictured were sent. Their relief at having left the *Kessel* is obvious but many suffered from feelings of guilt at having left their comrades behind.

A Red Air Force image of the devastation wrought in Stalingrad. This photograph was taken in February 1943 immediately following the German surrender.

Chuikov, with cigarette, and members of his staff on the banks of the Volga.

Out in the 'nose' of Stalingrad's western extremity, men of 3rd Motorized Division sit and wait for the inevitable Soviet attack. Leaving the fug of their dugout to fight was a huge physical and psychological effort. Once the defensive positions of this division were breached there was no alternative but to make for the city, surrender or die of exposure on the open steppe.

his wooden building has survived remarkably well considering everything that could be used for heating had been burnt. It is ossibly the HQ of one of the divisions to the south-west of the Mamayev Kurgan. The stereoscopic glasses were perfect for ootting movement on the barren snow. Soviet attacks were often led by men bearing the Red Flag and were not difficult to see.

With the Volga visible to the east the Red Flag signals the Soviet victory atop the Mamayev Kurgan.

A well-entrenched MG-34 position. Whiling away the hours in such conditions led men to fantasize. The rumour that an SS Panzer Corps was preparing a second relief mission was widespread and had some basis in truth. Hitler had ordered SS Panzer divisions to Kharkov, as Manstein was aware, but they were to be held in readiness for a counterstroke in the New Year.

An anti-tank unit of Don Front follows on the heels of the German retreat into the city. The gunners are passing a group of German dead. As the Sixth Army disintegrated, so more stragglers fell by the wayside. The treatment of POWs varied but the more cavalier Soviet attitude towards human life in general resulted in many being shot out of hand, the severely wounded in particular, as the Red Army had not always sufficient resources for its own men. The discovery of the appalling conditions in which Soviet POWs had been kept did nothing to mollify the ordinary Russians' attitude to the 'Fritzes' they captured.

The group of senior German officers, pictured here shortly after the surrender, includes von Seydlitz-Kurzbach (fourth from the left), who attempted to break out from the pocket on 23 November.

An Sd.Kfz 250 command vehicle negotiates a relatively unscathed part of the city, possibly a park or orchard. Some quartermasters had hoarded supplies for a day that never came and Soviet troops often found themselves the beneficiaries of such hidden treasures.

Here a column of Axis POWs crosses the frozen Volga River. For many it was the first and last sight of their objective that they would have. Over 90,000 men passed into Soviet hands. Roughly 5000 returned to their homes during the next fifteen years. Thousands were so malnourished that they died within days of capture.

Field Marshal Friedrich Paulus pictured hours after going into captivity. On 15 January he had been awarded the oak leaves to his Knight's Cross. Suffering from depression and dysentery, Paulus apologized to his captors for wearing his general's uniform as circumstances had made it impossible to alter it in line with his promotion on 31 January. Much to the chagrin of the men of Sixty-Second Army Paulus capitulated to an officer of Sixty-Fourth Army. They had hoped Chuikov would be able to accept his surrender as his men had borne the brunt of the city's defence. However, Chuikov did load and fire the first gun of the last barrage on 2 February.

The grisly harvest of Stalingrad: a field of Axis corpses on the outskirts of the city. Many have had their clothes and boots removed by civilians for their own use. In the background a GAZ lorry deposits another gruesome cargo.

One horse and one human survivor amidst the forest of chimney stacks, all that remain of an estate of wooden dwellings.

A troop of T-34s drives through the Red Square in Kharkov, the fourth city in the USSR. With the liberation of Kharkov Stalin anticipated the complete destruction of Army Group South. However, the Red Army was also at the end of its tether and supply chain, and now it was the turn of the Germans to restore their position east of the Dnieper River. In doing so they planted the seeds of their defeat at the battle of Kursk.

The captors of the of the Kalach bridge with General Rodin, commander of XXVI Tank Corps, on the right.

Vasily Zaitsev, the famous sniper, has his rifle inspected by Chuikov himself in January 1943.